T0315091

How to Develop a Sustainable Business School

How to Develop a Sustainable Business School

Véronique Ambrosini

Professor of Management, Monash University, Australia

Gavin Jack

Professor of Management, Monash University, Australia

Lisa Thomas

Professor of Strategy, Kedge Business School, France

Edward Elgar
PUBLISHING

Cheltenham, UK • Northampton, MA, USA

© Véronique Ambrosini, Gavin Jack and Lisa Thomas 2023

Published by
Edward Elgar Publishing Limited
The Lypiatts
15 Lansdown Road
Cheltenham
Glos GL50 2JA
UK

Edward Elgar Publishing, Inc.
William Pratt House
9 Dewey Court
Northampton
Massachusetts 01060
USA

Paperback edition 2024

A catalogue record for this book
is available from the British Library

Library of Congress Control Number: 2022948408

This book is available electronically in the **Elgar**online
Business subject collection
http://dx.doi.org/10.4337/9781802201215

ISBN 978 1 80220 120 8 (cased)
ISBN 978 1 80220 121 5 (eBook)
ISBN 978 1 0353 4057 6 (paperback)

Printed and bound by CPI Group (UK) Ltd, Croydon, CR0 4YY

Contents

Acknowledgements

This book builds on our research about the role of business schools and our passion for education and research. It is underpinned by our profound belief that sustainability and ethical behaviour should underpin what business schools do. Sustainability, equity and care for all stakeholders should be embedded within schools' operations, education and research. We hope that this book stimulates many conversations and, more importantly, fosters change.

We would like to thank Elgar's team for their support throughout this journey and especially Ellen Pearce, who helped us to initiate the project and kept us going through the ups and downs of academic life through the COVID-19 pandemic. We also thank all our colleagues, friends and family members who, knowingly or not, assisted us in developing our thoughts. Gavin would like to thank Eva Fisch and Jenny Fafeita, Monash University Library, for assisting with Chapter 4 material on Altmetrics.

Abbreviations

AACSB	Association to Advance Collegiate Schools of Business
ABDC	Australian Business Deans Council
AI	Artificial intelligence
AMBA	Association of MBAs
ARC	Australian Research Council
BARC	Building the Anti-Racist Classroom
BGA	Business Graduates Association
CABS	Chartered Association of Business Schools
COP26	United Nations Climate Change Conference, 26th conference
EDI	Equality/equity, diversity and inclusion
EFMD	European Foundation for Management Development
ERA	Excellence in Research for Australia
EU	European Union
FL	Futures Literacy
FoR	Field of research
FT	*Financial Times*
GEP	Gender Equality Plan
GRLI	Globally Responsible Leadership Initiative
HEI	Higher Education Institution
LEPs	Local enterprise partnerships
LGBTIQA+	Lesbian, gay, bisexual, transgender, intersex, queer/questioning, asexual
LSE	London School of Economics
MBA	Master in Business Administration

MENA	Middle East and North Africa
NGO	Non-governmental organization
NIT	National Interest Test
NTEU	National Tertiary Education Union
ORME	Organizing for responsible management education
PRME	Principles for responsible management education
REC	Race Equality Charter
REF	Research Excellence Framework
RIA	Research Impact Academy
RIL	Responsible individual learning
RMLE	Responsible management learning and education
RRBM	Responsible Research in Business and Management
ROL	Responsible organizational learning
RSM	Rotterdam School of Management
SDGs	Sustainable Development Goals
SMEs	Small and medium-sized enterprises
THE	*Times Higher Education*
THES	Times Higher Education Supplement
TRM	Teaching responsible management
UCEA	Universities and Colleges Employers Association
UKRI	UK Research and Innovation
ULSF	Association of University Leaders for a Sustainable Future
UN	United Nations
UNESCO	United Nations Educational, Scientific and Cultural Organization
UNGC	United Nations Global Compact
UoA	Unit of assessment

1. Introduction: business school context and globalization

There Are circa 16,000 business schools in the world (Hogan et al., 2021). In 2017, business school teaching revenues amounted to close to £400 billion, and 20 per cent of all students in higher education were attached to business schools (Parker, 2018). These figures highlight the significant role business schools play in society. While leaders and managers have a range of roles and embark on an infinity of tasks, one thing is sure: they make decisions that influence people, their community and the environment they operate in. They are instrumental to organizational success and the well-being of people and the planet. Hence their education is crucial. Business schools train many of the future leaders and managers of corporations and organizations in all sectors, be it for-profit or not-for-profit, governmental or non-governmental organizations, small or large, domestic or international. Business schools have an undeniable underpinning role in how future leaders and managers will behave. They can shape their worldviews. It means that they have a role in facilitating the United Nations Global Compact's goals. For the United Nations (UN), 'businesses are a force for good', and they contend that 'by committing to sustainability, business can take shared responsibility for achieving a better world' (UN Global Compact, 2021a).

In this book, we take a broad view of what sustainability means. We follow the UN's lead and consider the 17 Sustainable Development Goals (SDGs) as representing what sustainability includes. We do so as they have become the de facto embodiment of what sustainability signifies and is about (Moratis and Melissen, 2021). They represent three pillars of sustainability, that is, economic, environmental and social sustainability (Elkington, 1998). They encapsulate the Brundtland Commission's broad definition of sustainability as 'meeting the needs of the present without compromising the ability of future generations to meet their own needs' (WCED, 1987: 8). The 17 SDGs are: 1, No Poverty; 2, Zero Hunger; 3, Good Health and Well-being; 4, Quality Education; 5 Gender Equality; 6, Clean Water and Sanitation; 7,

Affordable and Clean Energy; 8 Decent Work and Economic Growth; 9, Industry, Innovation and Infrastructure; 10, Reducing Inequalities; 11, Sustainable Cities and Communities; 12, Responsible Consumption and Production; 13, Climate Action; 14, Life Below Water; 15, Life On Land; 16, Peace, Justice and Strong Institutions; and, 17, Partnerships for the Goals (UN Global Compact, 2021c). While we fully recognize that these goals are interrelated and of heightened importance, in this monograph, when dealing with business schools' operating model, we concentrate on those most salient to their ecosystem. These include quality education (4), gender equality (5) and partnerships for the goals (17). Of course, we do not privilege any SDG in regard to what business schools' curriculum should include. The curriculum should embed them all (Rusinko, 2010).

The UN call for businesses to align their 'strategies and operations with universal principles on human rights, labour, environment and anti-corruption, and take actions that advance societal goals' (UN Global Compact, 2021d). This is a tall order, but it is an imperative. Business schools need to act as organizations that become forces for good, and that embed the SDGs in their operations and develop the sustainability literacy of the leaders and managers they train. It means that business schools need to be aware of the implicit messages they send about sustainability through their institutional environment and values (Winter and Cotton, 2012) and through their curricula. All business schools' curricula need to embrace teaching and learning that enhance sustainability literacy. The teaching of sustainability needs to be holistic and cannot be silo teaching. It has to be interdisciplinary (Kurland et al., 2010), involving not only business, economics, marketing and management scholars but also experts in psychology, urban studies, ecology or sociology, to name just a few. It also requires educators and students alike to develop a passion for sustainability (Shrivastava, 2010). Educators need to think beyond hard scientific tools and techniques. They need to enthuse students and connect them emotionally and physically with the sustainability agenda. This is critical since, as Porritt (2005: xiii) argued, it is 'unreasonable to expect people to relate emotionally to long-term problems with which they feel they have little connection'.

A paradigm shift is needed; educators and students need to develop a sustainability mindset (GRLI, 2021a). This mindset shift includes understanding that, as mentioned, 'SDGs are deeply interconnected – a lack of progress on one goal hinders progress on others' (UN Global Compact, 2021c). Business schools need to be ruthless in the fight against the rhetoric that ecological and social sustainability come at the detriment of economic sustainability or that economic sustainability should be of primary concern. It also means understanding that one should dismiss the anthropocentric paradigm. Anthropocentrism supports the notion of human exemptionalism and the belief that the natural environment is a commodity for human beings to use and exploit (Borland et al., 2016). In its place, notions such as ecocentrism should become the dominant belief (Borland et al, 2016). It is about accepting that humans are simply one species amongst many, that all natural resources are finite and precious, and that the planet's homeostasis is the most critical consideration.

Sustainability literacy is broad. It encompasses elements such as developing students' awareness of the importance of environmental, social, political and economic contexts to their disciplines; building their understanding of what sustainable development is about and involves; raising their understanding of the contested issues related to sustainability; developing their attentiveness to cross- and interdisciplinary research; enhancing their critical thinking and reflexive learning; developing their sentience to the difficulty of decision-making given the complexity and non-linearity of the world and fostering their ability to comprehend, evaluate and adopt values conducive to sustainability (Dawe et al., 2005).

BUSINESS SCHOOL CONTEXT: COMPETITIVENESS AND STUDENT AND STAFF INTERNATIONALIZATION

The number, size and scope of business schools have expanded substantially over the last 50 years, and business schools have been susceptible to significant pressures to transform how they operate. Similar to other sectors, the drivers of this transformation are globalization, disruptive technologies, demographic shifts and deregulation (Friga et al., 2003). These factors have changed the nature of supply in the sector through the entry of new players nationally and globally (for example, the Huadu Business School in China). This more intense competition has led to some industry consolidation (for example, the merger of several business schools in France, such as Rouen and Reims), the formation of collaborative partnerships among institutions (for example, the partnership between Warwick (UK) and Monash (Australia)), and the increase in exchange programmes (for example, IESE with Berkeley, HEC, NUS) to better understand, respond to and align with changing stakeholder interests (Bolton and Nie, 2010). Similarly, the sector is witnessing changes in demand through changes in demographic cohorts in existing national markets and increased demand from international markets such as China or Brazil (Dhanaraj and Khanna, 2011). This is coupled with the search for and maximization of opportunities in new markets such as: online courses, be it online versions of traditional courses such as the MBA (Master in Business Administration) or MOOCs (massive open online courses); executive education programmes; and the launch of micro-credentials (micro-qualifications).

The globalization of the business school environment has changed its competitive dynamics. The competition for the best students, academic faculty, senior professional staff and research funding has intensified. It has also led to educational massification, focusing on operational efficiency and profit-margin optimization (McCulloch, 2009; Parker, 2013). This pressure has created a push towards larger class sizes, the removal of low priority or low number teaching units, and increased student–staff ratios (Parker, 2013). Some also argue that this has led to the decrease of academic standards and the reduction of subjects taught (Hogan et al., 2021). The reduction of government-funded research in many settings has also bolstered the search for an ever-increasing number of students. Many business schools rely on student revenue to fund their research endeavours, which is a means to ensure a presence in the rankings that business schools argue matters to students. This is, in effect, becoming an endless closed loop.

Students in business schools are international, especially in postgraduate studies. Many business schools have over 90 per cent international students in their classes for programmes such as their Master of Management or Master of International Business. Similar percentages can be found in global MBAs. For instance, according to Lister (2020), 96 per cent of the University of Edinburgh (UK) MBA students were international, for the ESSEC Business School (France) it was 98 per cent and for Rotterdam Business School (the Netherlands) it was 99 per cent. This means that business schools are becoming important players in their national economies. They generate billions in revenue from international students. For instance, altogether, in Australian universities, international student revenues amounted to 8.9 billion Australian dollars. Given that most international students take a business school course, business schools account for a large part of this income (Smyth, 2020).

Internationalization has become an imperative for business schools, with many universities relying on business schools' revenues to grow. This internationalization is not only driven by the quest for revenues, but also driven by accreditation bodies and rankings. For example, AMBA (the Association of MBAs) states that: 'In order to ensure programme diversity and sustainability, individual cohorts should be internationally diverse and balanced where possible. This is especially important for full-time programmes where the international experience offered by the MBA is an industry standard' (AMBA, 2019: 6). In the same vein, AACSB (the Association to Advance Collegiate Schools of Business) explains that: 'Graduates should be prepared to pursue business careers in a diverse global context. Students should be exposed to cultural practices different than their own' (AACSB, 2020: 16). Regarding rankings, the Financial Times (FT) MBA rankings have three measures of internationalization related to students: 'International students (4): calculated according to the diversity of current MBA students by citizenship and the percentage whose nationality differs from the country in which they study', 'International mobility (6): based on alumni citizenship and the countries where they worked before their MBA, on graduation and three years after' and 'International course experience (3): calculated according to whether the most recent graduating MBA class completed exchanges and company internships, lasting at least a month, in countries other than where the school is based' (Financial Times, 2021a).

The internationalization of business schools is not just about the internationalization of students. It is also reflected in business schools opening offshore campuses. So, for instance, Nottingham Business School operates in Ningbo, China; INSEAD in Singapore; and Monash Business School in Suzhou, China. It is also reflected in student exchange programmes, such as ERASMUS, which promote student mobility in Europe. Finally, business schools' internationalization is also a feature of business school staff. For instance, the IE Business School (Spain) and HEC Business School (France) teaching MBA faculty are 70 per cent international, and IMD Business School (Switzerland) 98% (Lister, 2020). This matters for ranking. For instance, the FT ranking of European business schools has a measure for the percentage of full-time academic staff whose citizenship is not that of the country of employment (Financial Times, 2021b). Of course, rankings are not the only reason for business schools to hire international staff; they also perceive that it is important to have international capability so that the international student population can receive a better education (Ryazanova and McNamara, 2019). This is only fostered for research purposes, as it helps research productivity thanks to knowledge sharing and transfer, and the development of skills via collaboration (Kim, 2017). The globalization phenomenon is not sustainability neutral. It has many implications, be it in terms of how business schools are run in regard to, for instance, their carbon footprint and its effect on climate change; their diversity and inclusion agenda; or what their students are being taught.

Now that we understand the environment business schools operate in, we can start tackling the drivers behind business schools adopting a sustainability agenda. This will provide us with the platform to subsequent chapters, recognizing that all are interlinked and that they take different angles on similar issues. We will consider first, in Chapter 2, 'Stakeholder engagement'. This chapter will look at stakeholder co-creation and partnerships for the SDGs. Second, in Chapter 3, we consider 'Responsible management and leadership education and learning'. This will directly deal with how business schools can develop ethical and responsible leaders. It will also cover pedagogical issues. Third, we will turn our attention to 'Research impact'. Chapter 4 addresses how business schools can modify their research agenda and broaden the scope of required outputs necessary to achieve their sustainability ambition. Chapter 5 is about 'Accreditations, rankings and business school governance'. We will suggest that to make the sustainability agenda a reality, business schools need to change, but so too do their institutional fields, which by and large govern or at least influence the way that business schools operate, including how they reward and recruit staff. Chapter 6 is about 'Equality/equity, diversity and inclusion' (EDI). It considers questions of gender and racial diversity and equality in relation to business school staff, students and curricula, and the global hierarchy of business schools. In our conclusion, we will reflect upon the advancement of technology in teaching and the acceleration in its use due to COVID-19. We will also address some of the implications of the global pandemic, climate change and the casualization of the academic workforce.

DRIVERS FOR ADOPTING A SUSTAINABILITY AGENDA

The context we described above has impacted business schools and the expectations and experiences of stakeholders. These stakeholders form a large group, and they are individuals, groups or institutions interested in or involved in business schools (Freeman and McVea, 2005). Business school stakeholders can broadly be seen to belong to four general categories (Ferlie et al., 2010; Finch et al., 2013; Thomas and Ambrosini, 2021): internal stakeholders (for example, teaching and research academics, deans, professional staff); practitioner stakeholders (for example, employing businesses); community stakeholders (for example, local governments, charities) and student stakeholders (students, alumni). Given the variety of contexts and the global and complex environments stakeholders may be engaged in, their actions and needs may be difficult to appreciate. This means that these stakeholders can be affected, positively or negatively, by what a school does. These stakeholders can also impact business schools in a variety of ways. This signals that different stakeholders will have various concerns, which may change over time and with experience. These stakeholders are core to understanding and addressing the challenges to the perceived value provided by business schools and the role of business schools. These stakeholders are critical drivers in business schools' pursuit of a sustainability agenda.

Criticisms of Business Schools

The diversity of stakeholders and competitive dynamics make the business school operating environment particularly challenging. Another factor is the large number of criticisms that business schools face on multiple fronts, be it from business and management scholars, business school leaders, the media, or industry and the professions. These criticisms include, for instance, the view that business schools have not changed their business models since the late 1950s, nor much of their teaching, meaning that, more often than not, students, and hence future leaders, are not accustomed to dealing with the pluralism of their stakeholders and privilege shareholders over others (Tufano, 2020).

The 2008 global financial crisis, which led to important questions being raised about the role of business and management education and the ethical norms taught in business schools, is arguably a consequence of such teaching (Pettigrew and Starkey, 2016). Business schools are seen by some to promote socially dysfunctional management models (Murillo and Vallentin, 2016), with a strong 'winner-takes-all' managerialist approach (Parker, 2018). The central theme of this critique is that teaching in business schools fosters the 'beating the competition' paradigm, lauds profit and wealth maximization, and emphasizes that human beings are driven by money, strategy is about manipulating an industry, and marketing is about exploiting customers. It extols the virtues of capitalist market managerialism (Parker, 2018). As early as 2005, Ghoshal eloquently explained that by teaching 'amoral theories, business schools have actively freed their students from any sense of moral responsibility' (2005: 76). Other, more general criticisms include not meeting the needs of students, by not adequately preparing them to address real-world management problems. Business schools are not always viewed as providing effective education, and that teaching and learning is often detached from the realities of management practice, undermining its relevance to industry (Pfeffer and Fong, 2004; Rubin and Dierdorff, 2013; Trank and Rynes, 2003).

Teaching is not the only source of critique of business schools. The way that scholars engage in research also gives rise to criticism. Tourish, in his book (2019) and in his polemic essay (2020), provides a scathing account, first, of journals publishing pretentious, unreadable and boring theoretical papers, and second, of researchers embracing an agenda devoid of any use for managers or students, and of questionable value for humanity and society at large. Researchers are encouraged by their institutions to write such papers as they are published in elite journals, key to rankings. He argues that 'we need more of what McKiernan and Tsui (2019) describe as *responsible management research*: that is, research that tackles important issues and seeks to make a difference' (Tourish, 2020: 107; emphasis in the original).

Altogether, these criticisms have eroded the level of trust bestowed on business schools. These examples illustrate why business schools can be accused of threatening well-being at individual, natural system, and community levels. It is argued by many, including us, that should business schools wish to remain relevant, they must become socially responsible (Akrivou and Bradbury-Huang, 2015). This implies embracing the SDGs.

Embracing the Sustainable Development Goals

An emphasis on business schools upholding social and ethical values so that they influence their students in their decisions to behave ethically (Hibbert and Cunliffe, 2015; Moosmayer, 2012; Nonet et al., 2016) and impact positively on society (Alajoutsijärvi et al., 2015) is reflected in accreditation bodies' visions for the role of business schools in society. For instance, the AACSB has drawn up a 'Collective vision for business education' that emphasizes the role of impact or engagement within the local and global community. Similarly, the European Foundation for Management Development (EFMD) stresses the need to promote an ethical view of business where sustainability should not simply be regarded as something added to the business school curriculum but as a constant consideration for the common good. The adherence by many business schools to the UN's Principles for Responsible Management Education (PRME) (as of 2021, 800 academic institutions from over 85 countries across the world have joined the PRME initiative) suggests that business schools are ready to accept the need to educate future ethical and responsible leaders. Signatories commit to transforming business and management education, advancing the SDGs, and educating responsible students with the ability to deliver on the SDGs in the future (UNPRME, 2021a). As stated, 'PRME engages business and management schools to ensure they provide future leaders with the skills needed to balance economic and sustainability goals' (UNPRME, 2021b). It continues: 'The PRME initiative was launched to nurture responsible leaders of the future. Never has this task been more important. Bold leadership and innovative thinking are needed to achieve the Sustainable Development Goals' (António Guterres, UN Secretary-General, cited in UNPRME, 2021b). Other initiatives such as the Globally Responsible Leadership Initiative (GRLI) share similar aims. GRLI focuses on catalysing 'the development of globally responsible leadership and practice in organizations and societies worldwide' (GRLI, 2021b).

PRME signatories are committed to six principles (UNPRME, 2021c). The first one is *purpose*: 'We will develop the capabilities of students to be future generators of sustainable value for business and society at large and to work for an inclusive and sustainable global economy.' The second is *values*: 'We will incorporate into our academic activities, curricula, and organisational practices the values of global social responsibility as portrayed in international initiatives such as the United Nations Global Compact.' The priority of the UN Global Compact is the achievement of the UN SDGs. The third is *method*: 'We will create educational frameworks, materials, processes and environments that enable effective learning experiences for responsible leadership.' The fourth is *research*: 'We will engage in conceptual and empirical research that advances our understanding about the role, dynamics, and impact of corporations in the creation of sustainable social, environmental and economic value'. The fifth is *partnership*: 'We will interact with managers of business corporations to extend our knowledge of their challenges in meeting social and environmental responsibilities and to explore jointly effective approaches to meeting these challenges.' Finally, the sixth is *dialog*: 'We will facilitate and support dialog and debate among educators, students, business, government, consumers, media, civil society organisations and other interested groups and stakeholders on critical issues related to global social responsibility and sustainability.'

The commitment to PRME and the ever-increasing interest in general sustainability – as highlighted by the coverage of COP26 (the 26th United Nations Climate Change Conference), reinforcing the importance of the international treaty on climate change (the Paris Agreement) – are not the only signals that underline the importance of sustainability issues for business schools. The presence of sustainability reporting in the press or in ranking systems is also a sign of the salience of these issues. The clear implication is that schools cannot set them aside. For instance, the Times Higher Education (THE) Impact Rankings assess universities against the SDGs. They compare them across four broad areas: research, stewardship, outreach and teaching. In short, the pressure and expectation that in the future business schools will need to accept the SDGs and make a positive impact on society, policy and practice is omnipresent.

This pressure is clear. The UN Secretary-General, António Guterres spoke at the 2020 World Leaders Forum on climate change and stated that the contributions of universities are essential to successfully addressing the climate crisis and realizing the UN's 17 SDGs. He concentrated on the importance for business schools to find and offer solutions to the SDGs' challenges (Symonds, 2021). This agenda is becoming more and more prominent. For instance, in a television documentary, Professor Robert MacIntosh, Chair of the Chartered Association of Business Schools (CABS) commented:

> In educating our students in making better decisions about the resources they use and the equality of the opportunities they create, our business schools shape the world in which we will live in the future. The world faces big challenges on climate and social inclusion, the answers to which don't just lie in technological innovation. Scientific breakthroughs are important but not enough on their own – they need an interface with business research to ensure their transition to viable products and services for the benefit of society. (CABS, 2021b)

Paul Polman, at the 2020 Responsible Research in Business and Management (RRBM) Summit, explained that 'the world is accelerating, and business schools need to move boundaries and create space for rapid change. Deans should look at drivers of behaviour, adding measures of societal impact of research to the current evaluation criteria' (Berry et al., 2021). In 2021, Berry also emphasized that:

> Business schools have always had the responsibility of preparing tomorrow's leaders. But today this is perhaps a greater responsibility than at any time in

history, given the herculean efforts needed to avert an apocalyptic future that nature never intended, and humankind never anticipated. There's reason to be hopeful for an alternative outcome – one where a circular or regenerative economy facilitates sustainable living; and our human and natural capital are equally valued – but it's far from guaranteed. Business schools are uniquely placed to help us build back better, and a good start would be to put public good at the heart of student learning and development. (CABS, 2021c)

The call for action is also clear in GRLI: 'As eight billion of us collectively press against multiple planetary boundaries, with associated challenges to societal and economic stability, the time has come to activate our global responsibility gene' (GRLI, 2021a). Assuming that there is indeed a genuine appetite for change from the business schools, this begs the question as to how business schools can embrace this agenda. This question pertains not only to their external stakeholders and educating their students and future leaders about the urgency and importance of dealing with the SDGs, but also to their internal stakeholders and the business schools' own modus operandi.

Business schools need to develop an agenda that purposefully promotes quality education, scholarly engagement, and valuable partnership relationships with diverse stakeholders to move forward. Accreditation bodies, governments and the media are also pushing this agenda. The expectation is that business schools will create more sustainable and positive impacts on society, policy and practice in the future by becoming more conscious of how they affect the world around them. As eloquently put by Starik et al. (2010: 377): 'While those of us in management education are certainly not solely, or even primarily, responsible for this bleak state of affairs, we have the opportunity to help lead our stakeholders, whether students, peers, alumni, or other collaborators, in the direction of significant and sustainable change.' Business schools cannot ignore the ecosystem in which they operate. The business world is progressively embracing the SDGs; and it started doing so before business schools did. Schools have to remain relevant and this is another driver, admittedly a push driver, but it is one. From large corporations, to small for-profit businesses, to social entrepreneurship organizations, the support for the SDGs is increasing. Many have strong goals and are visible in their actions. While greenwashing happens, more and more businesses expect their partners to be sustainability oriented. Examples of such companies include Voyageurs du Monde, a multinational tour operating firm with headquarters in France, which makes a strong case for dealing with only ethical companies or reducing their carbon print. This is epitomized by its chief executive officer (CEO) often saying that: 'Ecology will be the compass of tomorrow's travel' (Rial, 2021a), and 'Sustainable tourism is no longer an objective, but an absolute necessity' (Rial, 2021b). Even if the interest is slower than hoped, SDG investment increased tremendously in 2020 (World Economic Forum, 2021). These companies expect to deal with like-minded stakeholders. As such, if more and more organizations follow suit, and if business schools want to engage with them, they will have to change the way they operate.

The business world is not the only push driver. The future leaders are millennials and Generation Z, and they are concerned about climate change, social equality, and discrimination. They are ready to act when their values are not respected. 'They want a better planet, a fairer system, a kinder humanity—and they're ready to help make that happen, with small steps today giving way to giant steps as more millennials and Gen Zs assume positions of influence throughout society' (Deloitte, 2021: 5). Deloitte (2021: 33) continues that: 'These younger generations want to work for companies with a purpose beyond profit—companies that share their values—and that they feel more empowered to make a difference as part of organizations.' By implication, more and more students will demand an education that matches their ambition for a better world.

CONCLUSION

In this book, recognizing that change will not be straightforward or quick given the institutional forces at play, we argue that business school decision-makers need to examine and possibly re-create their visions of what the role of their business school is about. It means they will likely need to make choices in their sustainability journey, change their mindsets as to what their raison d'être is and appreciate the fundamental position of their stakeholders. This has implications, inter alia, for business school scholars who will need to be creative in recognizing and developing curricula for future ethical and accountable leaders. They need to modify their teaching and learning outcomes so that they are relevant to future leaders and managers, who will have to face an ever-changing and uncertain environment. These students will have to address the sustainability agenda in its myriad of dimensions. Very few students will be able to ignore the need for an inclusive and diverse workforce; very few will ever be able to consider that natural resources can be extracted and exploited without consequence for biodiversity and the planet; very few will be able to have non-transparent management practices that hinder the provision of decent work for all. In short, none will be able, as many have been so far, to dismiss the SDGs. In the following chapters, we address how business schools might move forward in their journey and develop a new modus operandi to embed sustainability. This will mean acknowledging a variety of important and interrelated topics within society, including economic, cultural, social and ecological factors, which we explore across the different chapters.

2. Stakeholder engagement

The business school environment is part of a broader educational institutional environment that includes industry, accreditation agencies, government organizations, commercial institutions and wider society. Despite the considerable changes that have taken place within business schools in recent years, substantial debate continues within the management education literature, with calls for more widespread change, innovation and redirection (Harrington et al., 2015). On the one hand, business schools are called to address the substantive concerns raised by the ongoing 'rigour and relevance' debate in management (Pfeffer and Fong, 2012; Rynes et al., 1999; Starkey and Madan, 2001) and flaws identified in current scholarly practices (teaching and research) (Antonacopoulou, 2010). On the other hand, there are important calls for Higher Education Institutions (HEIs) as social institutions to address sustainable development challenges towards the long-term public interest (Godemann et al., 2014). Since HEIs, and therefore business schools, shape human behaviour and cultural expectations, a more integrated approach to tackling sustainable development is needed (Godemann et al., 2014). Indeed, making practical contributions towards advancing both teaching and research that is committed to making a difference to the 'real world' through actionable knowledge is positioned as central to the agenda of supporting the co-creation of knowledge in management education (Antonacopoulou, 2010).

The 'rigour and relevance' debate in management education (Rynes, 2017; Starkey and Madan, 2001) has drawn attention to the need for management research to be more applicable to management practice and to be more reflective of the effects of research on life in organizations (Van de Ven and Johnson, 2006). Within this context, one recurrent argument is that business schools, primarily through their academics, must demonstrate their 'relevance' to secure their futures. But 'relevance' does not have to mean the pursuit of a narrow commercialization agenda where the business school becomes the 'servant' of industry, propagating a strictly managerialist view of the world (Bridgeman, 2007). Bartunek and Rynes (2014) refer to a series of tensions and paradoxes that underpin the rigour–relevance relationship. Narrow perspectives of such relevance (for example focusing solely on economic improvements for individual firms) hold the danger of neglecting wider impacts of academic interventions that may only become visible in the long run. As Hodgkinson and Rousseau (2009: 538) remark, there is a requirement to 'develop deep partnerships between academics and practitioners supported by appropriate training in theory and research methods which can yield outcomes that meet the twin imperatives of high-quality scholarship and social usefulness'. Consequently, in response to such critiques of the key activities of business schools, a more nuanced understanding of the rigour and relevance 'gap' is required where no one side of the relationship is dominant (Bartunek and Rynes, 2014; Anderson, Ellwood, and Coleman, 2017).

Another recurring argument directly linked to the rigour and relevance debate is that the current structure and models of management education are narrow, over-specialized and fail to provide students with the ability to relate to realistic management problem-solving situations (Khurana, 2007; Harrington et al., 2015). In the current business context, business schools have a key role in preparing graduates for positions that extend beyond those of subject specialist or technical expert (Harrington et al., 2015). They must support graduates to make a smooth transition to the workplace, bringing new ideas to the business and demonstrating an appetite for ongoing professional learning (Hynes and Richardson, 2007). This requires a greater exploration of the notions of 'employability' or 'industry readiness' of graduates, and an assessment of the attributes required of them to ensure that they are equipped to perform multifaceted roles in the workplace (Harrington et al., 2015). Further, business schools face the criticism that they have not been educating students for enough ethical reflection or any sense of broader responsibility (Borglund et al., 2019).

The business-as-usual approach which overemphasizes the basic activities of teaching, learning and research serves only to perpetuate an inward-looking business school. For example, it is now questionable whether it is sustainable or even acceptable to continue to invest in research driven primarily by scholarly interests unless economic, social, cultural, and political returns from investment in research are demonstrated. Consequently, a reassessment of activities of business schools is required, such that core functions can be strengthened to stimulate new activities and practices. For sustainable development, collaborative engagement can effectively stimulate new activities. As such, business schools must work with relevant stakeholders as part of wider stakeholder networks to support the achievement of sustainability objectives (Paucar-Caceres et al., 2022). This directs attention to a better appreciation of what impact may mean and how it may be delivered (see Chapter 4). Godemann et al. (2014) suggested that there are only a few groups of institutions that are placing sustainability as core to their teaching, research and operations. However, more recent research uncovered in the UK, for example through the CABS Taskforce Report 'Business schools and the public good' (CABS, 2021c), suggests the tide may be changing. This new tide suggests stakeholder engagement is becoming a key means of achieving business school missions which are increasingly focused on greater civic engagement.

STAKEHOLDER ENGAGEMENT AND SUSTAINABILITY

Stakeholders are key drivers of institutional change in higher education with impactful local and national networks (Paucar-Caceres et al., 2022). They are important to sustainability, which, in general, can be defined as linking the future quality of the global environment (environmental) to potential business opportunities (economic) through innovative and creative solutions which consider all stakeholders (social) (Zizka et al., 2021). Both internal and external stakeholders have an important role to play to support the achievement of sustainability objectives and behaviour change in the sector (Paucar-Caceres et al., 2022). Increasing interactions or partnerships around a mutually beneficial process of knowledge creation and exchange between the business school and external constituents represents a sustainable way forward for schools (Mtawa et al., 2016). Given some of the criticisms directed towards management education, stakeholder development for undertaking work in community contexts is a way of refuting any conceptualization of business schools as ivory towers. It becomes a means of showcasing a return to civic and public engagement (Renwick et al., 2020). Stakeholder engagement characterizes a more outward-facing approach of business school activities, in the way that they serve, partner or influence the community and/or the economy, either locally or in any specific location. While research and teaching continue to play a key role in this approach, greater stakeholder engagement for sustainability helps to refocus the primary outcome of activities towards a better functioning community or economy and broader society.

The call for wider engagement for sustainability within HEIs in general is not new, as is evidenced in this quotation from Boyer (1996: 18): 'The academy must become a more vigorous partner in the search for answers to our most pressing social, civic, economic and moral problems, and must affirm its holistic commitment to what I call the scholarship of engagement.' What is new is the potential role of stakeholder engagement for sustainability in the development of HEIs' future strategies, not least those of business schools. Stakeholder engagement is fundamental to achieving sustainability objectives as set, for example, in the mission of the Association of University Leaders for a Sustainable Future (ULSF, 2022a). This mission aims to support sustainability as a critical focus for teaching, research, operations and outreach at colleges and universities worldwide through publications, research and assessment. The initiative developed out of the Talloires Declaration (1990) (ULSF, 2022b), which set out a 10-point action plan committing institutions to sustainability and environmental literacy in teaching and practice. Later, the United Nations Decade of Education for Sustainable Development (2005–14) sought to mobilize the educational resources of the world to help create a more sustainable future (unesco.org/en). More recently, as mentioned in Chapter 1, initiatives such as the United Nations 2030 Agenda for Sustainable Development and the adoption of the 17 SDGs highlight the importance that various stakeholders beyond governments and policy-makers have in making efforts towards securing sustainability (https://sdgs.un.org/goals). The 2030 Agenda Partnership Accelerator represents the initiative aimed at accelerating and scaling up effective partnering across all stakeholders to deliver transformational impact for the SDGs. The PRME initiative sets out to achieve the sustainable development goals through implementation of the principles for responsible management education. Business schools are encouraged to foster and implement sustainable practices to fulfil these goals through modifications in curricula and research programmes (Fissi et al., 2021). All these initiatives have sought to make concerted efforts to shift the focus in business schools from merely learning to learning sustainably, and emphasize lifelong learning that will continue after the degree is granted. It is hoped that each decision graduates make subsequently within the workplace environment will have positive repercussions on society as a whole (Zizka et al., 2021).

Wider stakeholder engagement, collaboration and transparency are core to the business model of business schools and are an element which can represent a systematic approach to sustainability (Godemann et al., 2014; Paucar-Caceres et al., 2022). Additionally, the involvement of organizational members, including those often at the periphery of decision-making within business schools such as students and non-permanent, casual, or non-full-time faculty members, is important in processes of change via collaboration and shared leadership and transparency. Collaborative stakeholder engagement also serves to eliminate choosing one side of the rigour–relevance relationship, therefore creating the generative mechanisms for the co-production of knowledge and impact (Anderson et al., 2017; Bartunek and Rynes, 2014). High-quality interactions enable actors in collaborative relationships to co-create unique experiences that can be key to unlocking new sources of competitive advantage (Prahalad and Ramaswamy, 2004). Collaborative engagement has the dual benefit of informing and being informed by teaching, learning and research. As such, this engagement represents an important mechanism for providing business schools with opportunities to regain their legitimacy (Godemann et al., 2014).

FORMS OF STAKEHOLDER ENGAGEMENT

A holistic view of stakeholder engagement in the context of management education incorporates both internal and external parties in an integrated approach centred on a two-way flow of knowledge. Historically, approaches to engagement within HEIs have tended to fall under the umbrella term of 'community engagement' (Mtawa et al., 2016). Community engagement in higher education is described as incorporating sustainable networks, partnerships, communication media and activities between HEIs and communities at local, national, regional and international level (Jacob et al., 2015). The attention of institutions to community engagement has been largely founded on the work of Boyer (1990, 1996), in his response to growing criticisms of academic work that was self-referential and disconnected from the wider community and its needs (Renwick et al., 2020). For Boyer (1990, 1996), community engagement is a process which incorporates the exchange of knowledge between universities and communities through co-inquiry (jointly undertaking research activities) and co-learning. As such, core to community engagement were the two key activities of teaching and research. Boyer (1990) presented four forms of academic scholarship, namely the scholarship of discovery; the scholarship of integration; the scholarship of application; and the scholarship of teaching. He later added the scholarship of engagement to emphasize how engagement connects the four former dimensions of scholarship to the understanding and solving of pressing social, civic and ethical problems (Boyer, 1996). He stressed the need to broaden and deepen connections with community outside the academic domain. The intention was to ensure that academics' work is both created with and communicated to the public, and that it meets a public good (Renwick et al., 2016).

Over the last 30 years, community engagement has included an array of practices and partnerships which are not definitive but, rather, contextual, and are bounded by a business school's strategic framework, geographical location, capacity and related to their role within national policies (Mtawa et al., 2016). Examples of community engagement on the research side have variously been termed 'engaged scholarship' (Van de Ven, 2007), 'relational scholarship of integration' (Bartunek, 2007) or 'practice-relevant scholarship' (Antonacopoulou, 2010; Antonacopoulou et al., 2011). Engaged scholarship is a philosophy that highlights the importance of collaboration, a method 'in which researchers and practitioners coproduce knowledge' (Van de Ven and Johnson, 2006: 803). O'Meara and colleagues clarify that: 'Engaged scholarship conceptualizes "community groups" as all those outside of academe and requires shared authority at all stages of the research process from defining the research problem' (O'Meara et al., 2015: 3).

The idea behind engaged scholarship is the possibility of gaining a better understanding of complex social problems through many sources of knowledge by obtaining the advice and perspectives of key stakeholders (Van de Ven, 2007). It deals with complex issues with a long-term orientation often requiring diverse strategies for its execution. For internal stakeholders, this can involve crossing disciplinary lines (Hunt, 2008). Although scientific knowledge and practical knowledge are different, they can inform each other. It is felt that the greater embeddedness of the researcher in their contexts favours deeper insights and empathy for those they are researching, generating an immediate and multidimensional advancement of knowledge (Van de Ven, 2011). Examples of engaged scholarship evidencing differing levels of embeddedness include firms sponsoring research, practitioners co-authoring with faculty, or scientific collaboration between researchers from different institutions to pool knowledge in tackling complex problems, or as part of the conditions of funding agencies (Bozeman and Corley, 2004). However, while engaged scholarship has seen a resurgence in interest in recent years as a means of filling the rigour–relevance gap, there has been a tendency, upon implementation, to pay less attention to stakeholders' differing needs in their work contexts and for researchers to remain primarily discipline-based, conducting their research within silos. As such, it is suggested that there is some progress needed to turn concerns more towards contemporary sustainability concerns (Kitchener, 2019).

Community engagement on the teaching side frequently falls under the umbrella term of 'service learning'. Kenworthy-U'ren and Peterson (2005: 272) define service learning as 'creating opportunities for students to apply theory they learn in the classroom to real-world problems and real-world needs'. Often, these projects have the dual goals of developing critical leadership and teamwork skills, as well as promoting citizenship and social responsibility (Larson and Drexler, 2010). Faculty can help students to develop their technical skills while simultaneously helping them to develop greater interpersonal, intercultural and ethical sensitivity (Zlotkowski, 1996). For Zlotkowski (1996), service learning is characterized as a specialized form of internship. Students work within a setting established primarily to meet some social or community need (Larson and Drexler, 2010). Service learning provides a bridge between theory and practice in management education that has the potential to benefit students individually and society generally and is an academically rigorous instructional method that incorporates meaningful community service into the curriculum. Focusing on critical, reflective thinking and civic responsibility, service learning can involve students in organized community service that addresses local needs, whilst developing their academic skills, respect for others and commitment to the common good. Examples of service-learning encounters might include developing business plans and other strategies for non-profit organizations, working on a variety of social service projects for at-risk youths and/or economically disadvantaged citizens or creating a successful fundraiser for a non-profit organization (Harrington et al., 2015). Such initiatives are at the heart of the UN's 17 SDGs.

Within business schools, while service learning and engaged scholarship have historically tended to be unidirectional, limited and school-driven (Aguinis et al., 2019), they nonetheless attempt to engage with initiatives with the intention of greater societal impact and sustainable development. Nevertheless, more recent approaches are being evidenced which are providing a more purposeful and value-driven emphasis on engagement for addressing wider societal issues and to enhance the public good (Khurana, 2007).

THE PUBLIC VALUE MODEL

Thinking about public value is now at the forefront of cross-national discussion about the changing roles of the public, private and voluntary sectors in a period of profound political economic, ecological and social change (Bennington and Moore, 2011). The commitment of business schools to the public good combines both purposive action (movement away from the current instrumental rationality that pervades business schools) and substantively rational purposeful action (movement in a direction of travel informed by particular value commitments) (Kitchener and Delbridge, 2020). The approach draws on Brewer's (1983/2013) call for social science to combine features of scholarship to enhance public value. The Public Value Model embraces a focus on post-disciplinary approaches to producing scientific knowledge of relevance in addressing society's problems and active engagement within the civic and policy spheres (Kitchener, 2019). While concentrating specifically on public value, the goal is to achieve social amelioration and improvement in society, the market and the state (Kitchener, 2019; Price and Delbridge, 2015). Cardiff Business School in the UK has been recognized as the pioneer of this approach. It has implemented a progressive public value strategy, with principles committed to delivering economic and social improvement through interdisciplinary teaching and research that tackle contemporary grand challenges. The growing significance of the public good to universities is evidenced by the Impact Rankings, which are the only global performance tables that assess universities against the SDGs. The rankings provide comparison across four broad areas – research, stewardship, outreach and teaching – covering 1,118 universities from 94 countries/regions (timeshighereducation.com/impactrankings).

A key means of achieving public value is via stakeholder engagement initiatives. A business school committed to delivering public good develops a broader set of relationships across the public, private and third sector, including charities, social enterprises, and community groups (Brewer, 1983/2013; Moore, 2013; Price and Delbridge, 2015). This approach contrasts with narrower conceptions of impact (for example, those involved with REF, the UK Research Excellence Framework) (Kitchener, 2019); see Chapter 4. According to the CABS Taskforce Report (CABS, 2021c), the most commonly reported ways that business schools deliver public value through their external engagement activity include: student projects/internships in small and medium-sized enterprises (SMEs) and social purpose organizations; co-ordinating business networks and activities with an emphasis on underserved populations (for example women and ethnic minorities); public lectures; student volunteering; and various supports for local SMEs. At the same time, the report evidences more innovative engagement approaches, such as: partnerships with other education providers and Local Enterprise Partnerships (LEPs, in England); running pro bono law and business clinics; and enterprise support training targeted at deprived communities locally and internationally. Nevertheless, a one-size-fits-all approach to stakeholder engagement is not necessarily the way forward. As Kitchener and Delbridge (2020: 320) acknowledge, the Public Value Model 'is no panacea for all business schools' ills'. Further, as Kaplan (2018) points out, it may not be applicable across the full variety of schools operating globally.

However, collaborative approaches to stakeholder engagement can lead to the concurrent recognition of the potential of and opportunities for joint, reciprocal and other co-creative impacts between research and practice (Simsek et al., 2018). Additionally, a co-creation approach to external engagement assures that the business school's value proposition is what stakeholders are interested in and, at the same time, the business school benefits from the offer influenced by collaborators (Thomas and Ambrosini, 2021). Further, having industry partners serves to legitimize education in the eyes of other stakeholders and serves as a type of external facilitator or legitimizer (Borglund et al., 2019). Indeed, building longer-term, cross-sector and cross-disciplinary partnerships in the pursuit of a common mission not only enhances the skills of collaborators, but can secure improved employee engagement. Consequently, stakeholder engagement has the potential to both consolidate and extend value creation by engaging with a diverse set of stakeholder collaborators, including industry, the community at large and the public sector (Thomas and Ambrosini, 2021). Some promising examples serve to highlight the importance of wider stakeholder engagement for sustainability within business school models.

Some Positive Examples

The University of North Carolina (UNC) has been nationally recognized for its community engagement within all areas of scholarship (research/creative activities, teaching, service) for more than a decade. They are viewed as a pioneer for their active and intentional steps towards integrating community-engaged faculty work into promotion and tenure guidelines at university and department levels (Janke et al., 2014). While the UNC example presents success across all areas of community engagement, the CABS Taskforce Report (CABS, 2021c) breaks down examples into teaching and research. Promising examples within the UK environment which focus on teaching include Coventry Business School. The school promotes the positive values of ethics, responsibility and sustainability outcomes, supported via by real-world examples incorporated within the UN SDGs framework, across all its courses globally. A further example is presented at Edinburgh Business School, Heriot-Watt University, which has prioritized the delivery of the public good through flexible and accessible education over many years. Within its postgraduate teaching, it has been offering online education and distance learning since 1989. Recently, the institution has invested heavily in being at the forefront of educational practice and technology. The school believes that online working not only increases global reach, but also allows students to achieve their potential irrespective of their location, prior education or financial status, given the right support.

In terms of promising research-focused examples, Bath School of Management, University of Bath, focuses on sustainability through its Research4Good engagement initiative, which builds on a series of projects that investigate how research at the school can be translated into public good. For Lancaster University Management School (LUMS), social purpose lies at the core of their ethos, with the integration of the Work Foundation, a think tank that emphasizes social purpose, into the school.

Engaged scholarship is also included in the mission of some universities. For example, for the University of Memphis, engaged scholarship subsumes the scholarship of application. It adds to existing knowledge in the process of applying intellectual expertise to collaborative problem-solving with urban, regional, state, national and/or global communities and results in a written work shared with others in the discipline or field of study.

While it is encouraging to report on some promising examples of wider business school collaboration through different forms of stakeholder engagement, such engagement is not without its challenges. It is therefore worthwhile considering these if business schools are to move to incorporating such approaches within their models for future sustainability.

CHALLENGES TO STAKEHOLDER ENGAGEMENT

Despite a growing understanding of the importance of broader stakeholder engagement among business schools and its key role in sustainability, there are several tensions linked to wider implementation, not least related to the complexity of managing a wide variety of different stakeholders. Not all engagements between higher education and communities are positive, and collaborations can sometimes be unbalanced or one sided (Jacob et al., 2015). A lack of industry collaboration may be explained by inertia and resistance among business school professors who do not feel comfortable discussing major changes to their curricula (Rasche et al., 2012) and especially not with businesses (Borglund et al., 2019).

Additional areas of conflict relate to measuring the value of collaboration, for example, how can community-engaged scholarship be evaluated in ways that respect the growing spectrum of scholarship, while also preserving existing standards of high-quality scholarship? (Janke et al., 2014). Failing to evaluate collaborations means failing to appropriately recognize, reward and account for the full scope of faculty work, productivity and impact.

For academics, the challenges relate to developing and rewarding the capabilities and the sense of professional responsibility for contributing to transformations within schools (Dyllick, 2015). Failure to do so has the knock-on effects of poor support, difficulty in recruitment and retention of faculty members who are enthused by and contribute significantly to the public teaching and research mission and values.

Notwithstanding some promising emerging examples within business schools, as highlighted previously, these have tended to remain organic. This suggests a lack of appreciation among business schools of the need for a more strategic approach to external engagement (CABS, 2021c). Business schools should be more actively and intentionally seeking ways in which to strengthen their relationship and partnership opportunities. There are almost endless possibilities for positive engagement between higher education and communities; however, the future requires a more co-ordinated approach. As Kitchener and Delbridge (2020) state, business schools need to take more purposive action away from the traditional instrumental approach to strategy. This more purposive approach aligns with Thomas and Ambrosini's (2021) call for business school deans to focus on deepening and broadening engagement activity by changing their outcome-oriented strategic focus, conceding that the business school is not the sole provider of value, and helping to develop networks of collaborating stakeholders engaged in a process of mutual benefit.

CONCLUSION

The development of stakeholder engagement requires a new perspective and acceptance of a more porous set of relationships between teaching, research and service (Jacob et al., 2015). To better balance the different demands of knowing, doing and being, business schools need to develop and use to a much larger extent community engagement (or pedagogies of enactment), which requires students to enact their understanding and skills in extended, supervised practice (Dyllick, 2015). This poses implications for academics and their roles, as academics will need to transform from subject-matter experts to become facilitators or expert advisors who can provide knowledge and advice, or enablers of learning, who ensure that the learning environment is motivating, stimulating and conducive to learning (Dyllick, 2015).

Having the requisite resources to devote to wider stakeholder engagement is crucial. Business schools need to dedicate resources for the co-ordination and support of delivering public good through engagement. Such dedicated resources may include introducing an obligation in staff contracts to engage externally and establishing a senior academic school lead for engagement. Additionally, engagement relies on the collaborative teams being receptive to the knowledge and skills of others, and their being able to share these, to build trust and to have an open attitude towards change (Bobbink et al., 2016). This requires schools to move beyond just rewarding co-production (for example, income from the industry; the number of industry forums attended; or industry articles) and to incorporate criteria which relate to the achievement of direct project outcomes as perceived by the collaborators who are project beneficiaries (Thomas and Ambrosini, 2021). This approach is based on co-creation to ensure that the business school's value proposition is what stakeholders are interested in, and, at the same time, the business school benefits from the offer influenced by collaborators.

Parallel to these shifting perspectives, therefore, is the requirement for a shift in institutional policy and culture around rewards structures. The question arises as to how schools can adequately address the changing needs of students when institutional policies create disincentives for faculty members to undertake alternative forms of teaching, research, and service across their faculty roles. Scholarly products should reflect the evolving and dynamic nature of knowledge creation (Janke et al., 2014). New approaches which advance the scholarship of engagement will aim to incorporate revision of promotion and tenure guidelines, documenting scholarly engagement for reward systems and for improvement, and creating rigorous criteria for peer review of engaged scholarship (Sandmann, 2016). As the CABS Taskforce Report (CABS, 2021c) has outlined, today's graduate students and incoming junior faculty members self-identify as stronger scholars when they are actively participating in the making of a better world – they want to do work not only that pays, but also that matters.

In the future, business schools should be intimately established within their local communities to have a sustainable impact on society; likewise, local communities should have a seamless network with business schools to maintain an equal and positive partnership (Jacob et al., 2015). This implies first engagement with this community, and the need for constant efforts from both those within schools and external communities to maintain this important foundational community relationship.

3. Responsible management and leadership education and learning

The value of business schools today has been questioned from several different perspectives. Business schools and the business community at large seem to continue to be driven by a 'doing business as usual' paradigm that puts them at the periphery of complex global socioeconomic and environmental challenges (Gröschl and Gabaldon, 2018). This has profound implications when it comes to educating future leaders and decision-makers towards the greater requirement for them to lead in more responsible and sustainable ways. Yet, many participating in this traditional business model take operations for granted, emphasizing how far the current business school model has become institutionalized.

The evolving needs of the community and business stakeholders, and the changing nature of business careers, however, mean that business schools need to break away from outdated models and challenge the assumptions underlying their current activities (Currie et al., 2016). The global environment of new businesses, the active role of stakeholders, and the complex environmental and social challenges faced as communities transition to a more sustainable economic model require more pronounced interest in responsible leadership (Castillo et al., 2020). It seems that the warnings that schools should not take any future success for granted should now be heeded (Khurana, 2007; McGrath, 2007).

The time is ripe for greater recognition of the importance of integrating sustainability in business education to train the leaders needed by society in the present (Castillo et al., 2020). This is now more important, given that leadership is inseparable from a firm's capacity to contribute to the attainment of SDGs. Leadership is vital as it can have a direct impact on employees' attitudes and behaviours, whilst enhancing the firm's credibility among various stakeholders, given the symbolic nature of the leader who represents the business (Corriveau, 2020). Responsible leaders are required to act with integrity, in accordance with ethical values, and must create a climate of trust with subordinates and stakeholders that is conducive to the personal development of their collaborators and to organizational performance (Ortiz and Huber-Heim, 2017). The challenge of business schools of the future is to train the next generation of such responsible leaders.

RESPONSIBLE LEADERSHIP

The development of organizational changes towards more responsible and sustainable actions that address complex and pressing global socio-economic and environmental challenges will depend heavily on current and future business school graduates and on the business education that they receive (Gröschl and Gabaldon, 2018). The following definition of responsible leadership sets the scene for the requirements of responsible leadership education. Maak and Pless (2006: 103) define responsible leadership as 'a relational and ethical phenomenon, which occurs in social processes of interaction with those who affect or are affected by leadership and have a stake in the purpose and vision of the leadership relationship'. This definition places leader–stakeholder relationships at its core (Pless et al., 2011). Leaders' responsibility concerns influence over a broad set of stakeholders including clients, employees, the surrounding community and the natural environment (Cavagnaro and van der Zande, 2021). Indeed, a common denominator in conceptualizations and definitions of responsible leadership is accountability to different stakeholder groups (Voegtlin et al., 2020).

According to Voegtlin et al. (2020), this requires leaders play three key roles: being an expert for multiple stakeholders through setting tasks and achieving performance goals; being a facilitator through motivating employees and creating a fair work environment; and, further, being a citizen with a focus on wider stakeholders, such as non-governmental organizations (NGOs), community, state and family, with a view to creating long-term value for society. Consequently, responsible leadership requires an understanding of the business–society relationship, but also a moral sensitivity for the impact of business on society and the environment, and an appreciation of the centrality of ethics in business decisions and behaviours (Smit, 2013).

Such descriptions of responsible leadership have core implications for management education (Moser, 2021). The educational challenge of developing globally responsible leaders centres on developing the potential of individuals to act consistently on behalf of society, such that they develop the ability to embrace complex transdisciplinary issues and capabilities for hands-on collaboration with other members of the larger community (Muff, 2013).

RESPONSIBLE MANAGEMENT AND LEADERSHIP EDUCATION AND LEARNING

The United Nations Global Compact (UNGC) has stimulated a movement that has led to new thinking about the role of business in society, as well as the role of management education (Smit, 2013). Business is asked to embrace, support and enact, within its sphere of influence, a set of core values in the areas of human rights, labour standards, the environment, and anti-corruption (Rasche and Kell, 2010; Smit, 2013). This subsequently led to the establishment of the GRLI and, secondly, the PRME, which we introduced in Chapter 1. However, a fundamental question arises as to the kind of management education that will be most conducive to developing managers who are able to exercise business leadership that will be regarded as ethical and responsible in the context of a sustainability-challenged 21st-century society (Smit, 2013). What is clear is that traditional educational programmes and initiatives, as well as manager roles, are being questioned. Today leader and manager roles with different priorities and values are required in face of the multiple challenges in the current environment (Gröschl and Gabandon, 2018). The educational challenge is to develop the potential of individuals to act in a reflective way on complex and controversial issues and in collaboration with different stakeholders (Dyllick, 2015). Education should help students to make sense of this world and their place in it and instil in them a sense of responsibility for the common good (Muff, 2013). In confronting these challenges, business schools, through their provision of responsible management education, not only contribute to the possibility of significantly contributing to creating win–win situations for organizations and their stakeholders, but also help to address the challenges of organizing for corporate social responsibility (CSR) (Voegtlin et al., 2020). In so doing, they maintain their own legitimacy.

FOUR CATEGORIES OF RESPONSIBLE LEADERSHIP IN TEACHING AND LEARNING

Within the realm of responsible management learning and education (RMLE), research into responsible leadership has been separated into four distinct categories: teaching responsible management; organizing

Table 3.1   *Four categories of responsible leadership in teaching and learning*

	Provider-centric	Learner-centric
Individual level	**Teaching responsible management** Main focus on faculty as individual providers of RMLE. Focus on the role of pedagogical approaches, evaluation and assessment, and taught content	**Responsible individual learning** Main focus on the individual learner. Explores processes which influence how students and managers learn responsibility
Organizational level	**Organizing for responsible management education** Main focus on business schools and other institutional providers for RMLE. Explores issues related to developing RMLE as an organizational capacity among providers	**Responsible organisational learning** Main focus on workplace/ organization as the learner. Explores processes of RMLE and change at group level

Source: Adapted from Cullen, J.G. (2020). Varieties of responsible management learning: A review, typology and research agenda. *Journal of Business Ethics*, 162: 759–773.

for responsible education; responsible individual learning; and responsible organizational learning (Cullen, 2020). These categories are depicted in Table 3.1.

Cullen's (2020) systematic review of the RMLE literature demonstrates that: the category of *teaching responsible management* (TRM) explores the teaching activities of individual teachers, most often research by the teachers themselves; *organizing for responsible management education* (ORME) largely discusses the implementation of PRME in business schools; *responsible individual learning* (RIL) mainly researches how students learn about responsibility; *responsible organizational learning* (ROL) is concerned with how organizations, and groups of managers within organizations, may learn and change in socially and environmentally responsible ways (for a full assessment of each category, see Cullen, 2020). The study concluded that there is a much greater volume of provider-centric compared to learner-centric research, and that ROL is the most under-studied and untheorized category of RMLE. It also found that there is still a need for conceptual and empirical work on how managers learn responsibly in their own organizational context. However, returning to the definition and descriptions of responsible leadership as outlined earlier in the chapter, regardless of the category of responsible leadership teaching and learning emphasized, what will act as a foundation across all categories is the acknowledgement of two important underlying dimensions to future business school sustainability and therefore future-relevant teaching and learning approaches. These dimensions relate to the requirement for greater stakeholder engagement (see Chapter 2) and therefore collaboration, and the pull towards the need for greater transdisciplinarity and systemic approaches to problem-solving.

TRANSFORMATION TO GREATER COLLABORATION AND TRANSDISCIPLINARITY

The emerging field of responsible management learning is characterized by an urgent need for transdisciplinary practices (Laasch et al., 2020). Engaging in RMLE is a complex task and cannot be achieved by relying on individual disciplines and sectors of knowledge (Laasch et al., 2020). It requires a different perspective on knowledge integration from the disciplines of ethics, responsibility and sustainability, as well as from other academic and business management sectors (Laasch and Moosmayer, 2015). Indeed, such management learning and education needs to reflect the conflicting or contradicting stakeholder interests beyond and outside traditional organizational boundaries, necessitating the ability of future leaders to deal with moral dilemmas and the capacity to behave in fair and ethical ways (Muff et al., 2020). It not only requires a key emphasis on developing the competencies required for individual learning for responsible leadership, but also the importance of collaborative competencies such as those required to engage effectively with experts and stakeholders, through facilitating participatory research and collaborative decision-making (Ortiz and Huber-Heim, 2017).

Business school curricula continue to be largely characterized by their separation of disciplines, by their focus on isolated disciplinary knowledge delivery and disciplinary problem orientation in the classroom, and by their strong scientific approaches in the context of business school teaching and research (Gröschl and Gabaldon, 2018; Khurana and Spender, 2012; Pfeffer and Fong, 2012). This separation of disciplines, coupled with an emphasis on analytical thinking, has created a reductionist approach to problem-solving that promotes dualistic thinking amongst students, preventing them from being able to address complex phenomena in any holistic manner and vice versa (Gröschl and Gabaldon, 2018).

Yet, the problems of practice are rarely discipline-based (Starkey and Madan, 2001).

Transdisciplinarity, whether this be in teaching and learning, in research or through professional practice, relies on collaborative practices in attending to complex issues, by integrating knowledge from multiple disciplines and sectors (Kurland et al., 2010; Laasch et al., 2020). Societal problems become the shared research object that unifies and co-ordinates the disciplines (for example, biology, psychology, economics disciplines) and sectors (for example, academic, business, government sectors (Laasch et al., 2020). Consequently, collaborative transdisciplinary practices integrate disciplinary knowledge (interdisciplinarity) and sectoral knowledge (intersectorality) for solving shared complex overarching problems. Transdisciplinarity also requires collaborating intersectorally (collaboration across sectors) by bridging academia–management boundaries (beyond disciplinary boundaries), integrating knowledge on both sides of 'the great divide' (Laasch et al., 2020; Rynes et al., 2001).

In order to understand the emerging business challenges and opportunities, within models of responsible management and leadership, focus needs to be placed on societal, environmental and economic issues and their interconnectivity in order to develop an ability to lead complex decision-making processes in collaboration with societal stakeholders (Muff, 2013). We are already seeing examples of approaches within higher education institutions which embrace the need for greater transdisciplinarity. The Université Côte d'Azur, France, for example, has initiated a unique programme that brings together multidisciplinary student teams to meet and overcome real challenges that have been identified by public sector partners. In four years, they have carried out more than 30 student partner creation projects focusing on problems within the local community and society.

However, transdisciplinarity is not necessarily a substitute approach or one that should dominate, but instead can complement a disciplinary approach (Gröschl and Gabaldon, 2018). It reflects an additional underpinning component of responsible management education (Laasch et al., 2020). Nevertheless, becoming transdisciplinary poses challenges for learners, with implications for business school education. Such collaboration practices with a broad set of stakeholders requires an ability for broader collaboration competencies (Muff et al., 2020). Consequently, the requirement is for the development of a holistic skillset for the future manager, be they an educational manager or the next leader of a Fortune

500 company. This will call for business schools to emphasize approaches for embracing transdisciplinarity in developing the responsible leaders of tomorrow. To this end they need to develop environments conducive to responsible management learning and leadership, such that learners are comfortable with complexity and uncertainty for future decision-making, and to encourage learners to draw on personal reflection enabling them to critique the assumptions upon which their beliefs have been built (Malkki, 2010). The following represent examples of such environments and capabilities, and techniques which are, in the main, aligned to PRME Principle 3 – Method: 'We will create educational frameworks, materials, processes and environments that enable effective learning experiences for responsible leadership'.

Developing Environments and Contexts for Responsible Management Learning

Clearly, leaders do not emerge from a vacuum; rather, individuals develop into leaders. If we want to have the leaders required by society, we must promote optimum environments for their development, in the most direct or proximal context. This context will necessitate greater collaboration with multiple stakeholders both external and internal to the business school.

Transdisciplinary education is centred on globally and locally issue-centred learning (Muff, 2013), or complex real-life problems which aim to prepare professionals or to enable other actors across society to produce problem-solving knowledge (Laasch et al., 2020). It means encouraging faculty from different disciplines to collaboratively teach courses and programmes that are inquiry-driven rather than discipline-driven and that focus on broader fundamental questions, and complex challenges that business leaders currently face (Gröschl and Gabaldon, 2018). Faculty as facilitators of learning should foster systemic perspectives on a subject of inquiry that help students to learn to connect seemingly contradictory and opposing concepts and ideas, and that challenge students in their sense-making of parts and the whole that define complexities that they will face as future business leaders (Gröschl and Gabaldon, 2018; Moon, Walmsley, and Apostolopoulos, 2018). Anticipating implications and consequences across multiple complex systems requires students to be comfortable in systemic thinking, and to develop their skills for breaking down complexity (Muff, 2013). Responsiveness to a shifting context is a critical skill for good leadership.

Consequently, academics will need themselves to become comfortable with diversity, recognizing assumptions and prejudices, and generating within the organization a sense of generosity to different points of view (Stokes and Dopson, 2020).

However, the same context requires business schools to offer valuable opportunities to undergo formative and significant experiences that contribute to building the motivational drivers of responsible leadership (Castillo et al., 2020). It requires the co-ordination of sustainability courses within curricula, and their integration in general introductory courses for undergraduate degrees, as well as opportunities for collaborative research between academic researchers and practitioners as critical success factors of real-world learning opportunities in the field of sustainability (Ortiz and Huber-Heim, 2017). Additionally, in terms of programme and curriculum development, from a design point of view it is important to decide which subjects should be treated in depth and will thus receive modular status, and which ones should be treated as cross-cutting and should thus be incorporated into everything else (Smit, 2013). We might also add that it is important to be aware of what is not formally designed into our programmes or curricula, since educators communicate social and behavioural expectations to their students and set a tone for ethical and social interactions in the classroom and beyond, regardless of whether they have planned to do so or not (Moser, 2021).

The sustainable business school should acknowledge the importance of fostering the development of the individual's ability to perceive the needs of others (based on his or her empathy), and the compulsion to consider those needs relevant to values (congruence with personal values, positive affect) that drive perceptions of responsibility for multiple stakeholders and, subsequently, the performance of aspects fundamental to responsible leadership (Castillo et al., 2020; Voegtlin et al., 2020). It means experiencing live environments where students can develop these abilities. Responsible leadership needs to be congruent with the learner's proximal environments (Castillo et al., 2020). This requires developing opportunities for leaders in training, at undergraduate and graduate level, to feel responsible by being exposed to transformative experiences where they are allowed to participate in their social environment, assume the roles of others and place themselves in the others' context (Corriveau, 2020; Castillo et al., 2020). Examples of such contextual experiences could include contact (share/live) with communities in need, and having to deal daily with the consequences/externalities in economic, environmental and social terms associated with business decisions (Castillo et al., 2020). Such opportunities allow the individual to live a concrete experience in a context that will be physically, mentally or emotionally challenging (Corriveau, 2020). A well-designed experiential learning programme that includes significant trigger events and sufficient spaces for reflexivity contributes to self-awareness that fosters individuals' personal and professional development (Awaysheh and Bonfiglio, 2017).

The Experiential Learning Design Accelerator (the Accelerator) at the University of Arizona builds on the vision of '100% Engagement' by directly supporting faculty with dedicated time, space and community to design courses that integrate community-based experiential learning for undergraduate students. The Accelerator provides mentorship from academics who are actively practising engaged learning pedagogy. It also provides support for developing and sustaining campus, community or employer partnerships, as well as training in human-centred design and iterative problem-solving as it applies to course design. Financial incentives for faculty and community partners to complete course design are also provided.

The creation of such experiential learning opportunities has implications for business schools insofar as it will require the creation of new learning spaces such as transdisciplinary 'ateliers' either inside or outside the business school. This may also include cyberspace, where transdisciplinary teams are jointly collaborating in learning how to solve real-live problems (Laasch et al., 2020).

Developing Futures Literacy

In order to make decisions that embrace complexity, responsible leadership requires that uncertainty be treated as a resource, not an enemy. This calls for a significantly enhanced capacity to use the future to understand the present. RMLE means developing new approaches to advance innovative thinking and creative solutions to develop the competences to address the world's complex wicked problems. Building this greater capacity rests on bringing anticipation out into the open as the way the future exists in the present (Cagnin, 2018). Futures literacy (FL) provides such capacity. FL is a capability to know how to imagine the future (Larsen and Kæseler-Mortensen, 2020). It is the skill that allows people to better understand the role of the future in what they see and do. Being futures literate empowers the imagination and enhances an ability to prepare, recover and invent as changes occur (UNESCO, 2021). This ability is acquired by undergoing a process of learning-by doing (Miller, 2007), to reveal and challenge the implicit and explicit anticipatory assumptions we use to think about the future. Participants of such processes engage in a simulation that advances their capacity to make strategic decisions in contexts of ambiguity by more fully exploring the potential of the present. In this manner, diversity and complexity can serve as sources of inspiration (Miller, 2010). Futures-literate persons demonstrate the skills needed to decide why and how to use their imagination to introduce the non-existent future into the present (Miller, 2018). It is a skill or ability to harness the power of images of the future, to enable us to more fully appreciate the diversity of both the world around us and the choices we make (Larsen and Kæseler Mortensen, 2020).

However, within many existing degree programmes in leadership and business management, foresight theories and tools for developing future literacy and opportunities for practice are largely absent or at best, nascent. Nevertheless, there are a number of universities and business schools which are embracing this approach to skill development. Loes Damhof, Senior Lecturer in 21st-Century Skills, UNESCO Chair in Futures Literacy, at the Hanze University of Applied Sciences in Groningen, the Netherlands, develops futures literacy capability within the curriculum for master's-level students as well as in training modules for those faculty teaching such master's-level courses. Both students and faculty not only learn the capability, but also learn how to design and facilitate Futures Literacy Laboratories to apply futures literacy in their studies and workplace. These laboratories are designed to challenge thought patterns among learners, such that futures literacy can change the conditions of change. This is suggested as an important requirement for guiding transition processes in society and businesses.

Indeed, a number of other universities around the world now have programmes of study dedicated to developing futures literacy among learners. For example, the University of Stellenbosch (Business School) in South Africa has a programme on Futurism and Business: Dealing with Complexity; Regent University, USA, has developed an MA in Organizational Leadership – Futures Studies; Aarhus University/ Department of Management, Denmark, has an MA in Future-Oriented Strategizing; and Swinburne University of Technology, Australia, has developed an MA in Foresight Knowledge and Methods.

Developing Learner Reflection

At the individual learner level, reflection is placed as central to what an individual has done in the past and how this informs where they intend to go in the future. Such reflection enables a critique of the assumptions upon which our beliefs have been built (Malkki, 2010). It allows individuals to undertake a process of making new or revised interpretations of the meanings of experiences, consequently underpinning further interpretation in future experiences (Mezirow, 2000).

In developing responsible leaders, critical reflection is an important capability to cultivate. This might start by encouraging students to (un/re) learn to ask questions, engaging students in debates, dialogues and other exchanges that foster curiosity, reflection, understanding, openness and toleration (Morin, 2014). However, self-reflection should not stop with students. Faculty members' efforts to transform and constantly educate themselves by taking into account real socioeconomic and environmental problems should be an integrated objective of business schools (Gröschl and Gabaldon, 2018). It invites personal change and learning amongst actors as part of their ongoing practice (Antonacopoulou, 2010).

Given that self-awareness and solid moral foundations are central to responsible leadership, teaching approaches that promote reflexivity, such as experiential learning, should be privileged; an example might be coaching for the development of components associated with authentic leadership (Corriveau, 2020). The process of recreating and legitimizing new and more responsible forms of management education such as those outlined here and reflected within PRME Principle 3 rely on praxis (Verbos and Humphries, 2015). Praxis is the outcome of a dynamic relationship between action and reflection. Trusting relationships developed through praxis between individuals or stakeholders enables co-creation and choice among available possibilities. This provokes an ability for change (Verbos and Humphries, 2015), and we might argue that this change will stimulate a break from currently entrenched institutional practices of business schools towards embracing new methods for developing responsible leaders so that they may better serve their futures.

Organizing for Responsible Management Learning and Education

What emerges from an exploration of the sustainable business school of the future is that such a school understands that transforming business, the economy and society starts at home with its own internal transformation (Muff, 2013). It does so through embracing the need to transform operations and practices in a transparent and inclusive manner. It requires a more holistic view on how the integration of responsible management education can be organized (Solitander et al., 2012).

The reach of business schools is unprecedented, with millions of undergraduate and graduate students as well as professional leaders engaging in leadership and executive training at business schools (Morsing, 2021). By signing up to PRME, business schools commit to integrating the idea of responsible management not only in their research, teaching and relations with different stakeholders but also in their own organization. Given that social and environmental challenges as well as stakeholders' expectations change over time, PRME supposes an ongoing learning process (Solitander et al., 2012). This means the response from business schools should not simply be about keeping the status quo, but rather transforming into a new state in relation to the changing societal context and expectations. The recent name change of Cass Business School, now Bayes Business School, London. serves as an example of a willingness to transform. As their website (https://www.bayes.city.ac.uk/about/more/our-name-change) explains,

> In 2001, we accepted a large donation to fund our new building and agreed to adopt Sir John Cass's name. We researched the Sir John Cass Foundation, which funds educational opportunities for underprivileged communities in East London. We regretfully did not look at the man who was the source of the Foundation's wealth, and what taking his name might imply. Our name signals who we value and whose voice we judge as worthy of being heard. Sir John Cass worked directly for The Royal African Company, which was set up to organise and profit from the Atlantic slave trade.
>
> Neither Cass's philanthropy nor the passage of time will erase the suffering he caused and the persisting inequality that slavery has contributed to creating in the UK and across the world. The exploitation of others through seemingly legitimate business practices remains a source of wealth for many individuals and corporations. As a Business School, we have a role to play in addressing this. Rejecting the name of a slave trader is a first step in that direction.

There is also a need to challenge some past and current recruitment and selection profiles of business school staff. Accepting non-traditional business school academic profiles, professors with liberal arts degrees and with backgrounds in philosophy, literature and history could help bridge cultures of science and humanism (Gröschl and Gabaldon, 2018). Any move towards more transdisciplinary-oriented thinking amongst business school educators will also require changing the structures and contexts in which business school educators work (Thomas and Ambrosini, 2021).

For faculty engagement, there needs to be a willingness to engage actively with transdisciplinarity. As outlined in Chapter 2, academics need to be encouraged to transform their practice by working across boundaries where their interests in selected theories and paradigms are open to being challenged in an integrative space. PRME supports intentionally general principles, inviting a contextual space for each academic institution to develop its own meaning, sharing ideas, and for best practices to diffuse throughout business curricula, considering regional or local differences (Rasche and Escudero, 2010).

As outlined at the beginning of the chapter, this transformation represents a challenge when current business school models promote a system that rewards individual teaching and research performance, rather than the time and effort spent at the interface of collective and integrative work. However, business schools can no longer pursue a business-as-usual approach within an ecosystem that reinforces stability and rewards continuity, where programmes are created, faculty members are recruited and where much investment is made in marketing to scale the ranking systems, since the stakes for the future are not just financial (Bouchikhi and Kimberly, 2016; Smit, 2013). Transformation is only possible if faculty members are themselves convinced that changes must occur in business schools in order to tackle the complex global economic, social and environmental problems (Gröschl and Gabaldon, 2018). This is important for any consideration of the development of responsible management teaching and learning.

CONCLUSION

Achieving the SDGs by fully adopting the PRME will not be an easy task. It involves changing the mindset of current and future managers such that they adopt a global and ethical perspective on their decisions and actions. To this end, management education has a key role to play in developing learners who question their values, learn to take other people's views into account in their decisions, are transparent and prepared to develop a strong moral ethic. To stimulate such sustainable and responsible education, a renewed focus on business school governance to develop impact through ethical and sustainability education and practice is imperative. It will require a shift from 'teaching' students to supporting students, 'enabling' the leaders and managers of tomorrow to learn applied skills of relevance to business and society in general (Moon et al., 2018). In a future which calls for multiple and more intense relationships with stakeholders, a context which goes hand in hand with a need for transdisciplinarity, greater attention to relational ethics will highlight contradictions in the current role of business schools which may bring transformational opportunities for those willing to engage with them. This will be the stimulant to transform the present business school institutional order, resolving their limitations and yet retaining benefits where they are deemed to remain desirable (Verbos and Humphries, 2015).

4.   Research impact

This chapter addresses how business schools can modify their research agenda and broaden the scope of required outputs necessary to achieve their sustainability ambition by embracing a research impact agenda. The argument here is that generating and communicating research impact represents one important way for researchers and business schools to deliver on the SDGs. By research impact, we are primarily referring to the outcomes and effects that follow the use, implementation, adoption or adaptation of academic research by those outside academia (sometimes referred to as 'societal impact'). The Australian Research Council (ARC) gives examples of research impact as: research influencing a policy position; improved business performance; more effective management or workplace practices; reduction in production costs; creation of a social enterprise (and thus jobs); changes to regulations; or the commercialization of a new product. This is distinct from notions of impact as the use or influence of academic research within disciplinary fields (sometimes referred to as 'scholarly impact'), as measured for example by journal article citations or peer reviews.

There is much to be done, however, to transform business school research efforts into impactful sustainable outcomes for stakeholders beyond the university (for example, private/public/third sector organizations; government bodies or policy-makers; individual managers; consumer or pressure groups; social movements; or the natural environment). As we will also highlight in Chapter 5, the status quo of many business schools prioritizes publications in a limited set of typically English-language academic journals as the key proxy for research achievement. Academic efforts and business school recruitment and reward systems are thus understandably often focused on being published in these outlets as a valuable and worthful outcome in and of itself. That academic research can and should have a life and a value beyond its appearance in academic outlets is a longstanding refrain of those calling for management research that is rigorous, relevant and makes a difference (AACSB, 2021a; Rynes, 2017; Shapiro and Kirkman, 2018; Sharma and Bansal, 2020). This is becoming more pressing as a set of drivers external to business schools globally places greater pressure on business schools to deliver impacts beyond academia.

In Australia, La Trobe University's research impact strategy document makes the imperative clear: 'We must keep pace with government and community expectations that publicly-funded research yields direct public benefit.' Many national grant-funding bodies, for example, now require applicants to explain their so-called pathways to impact, that is, how they will translate their research into positive societal outcomes for research end users and other named stakeholders. The ARC introduced a National Interest Test (NIT) in 2018 into some of its national competitive grants programmes. The ARC notes that 'the purpose of the NIT is to demonstrate the societal benefits (economic, commercial, environmental, social and/or cultural) of the proposed research beyond the academic community. The audience of the NIT is the general public …' (arc .gov.au/funding-research/apply-funding/grant-application/articulating -national-interest-grant-applications).

Some national research assessment exercises (for example, the REF in the UK, or Excellence in Research for Australia (ERA) in Australia) now include research impact (using different definitions and parameters) in their evaluations. The UK REF was the first to do so, defining research impact as 'an effect on, change or benefit to the economy, society, culture, public policy or services, health, the environment or quality of life, beyond academia' (ukri.org/about-us/research-england/research -excellence/ref-impact/). In 2014, UK institutions of higher education put in 6,975 impact case studies for assessment.

All business schools seeking (re-)accreditation from the AACSB are required to demonstrate evidence of how they meet key business standards, including Standard 8 on 'impact of scholarship', and Standard 9 on 'engagement and *positive* societal impact' (emphasis added). While the first relates to the 'production, dissemination, and impact of a school's thought leadership as it relates to scholarship', the second one is focused on 'a school's engagement with and impact on society' (AACSB, 2020a: 49). The normative emphasis in Standard 9 on 'positive' societal impact, arguably implicit in all definitions of impact, gestures at the possibility that some research impacts could be negative, and so suggests the moral and political nature of this phenomenon.

Impact is thus very much on the agenda of the contemporary business school in a variety of locations including Australia, Canada, New Zealand and the UK. Yet the question of how academic work would come to be engaged with, understood, adopted or used by external stakeholders so as to make a positive and sustainable societal impact is a complicated one. There is no easy recipe for researchers to follow for research impact, nor a one-size-fits-all approach for business schools to support researchers towards this goal. We consider that such ambiguity is potentially productive for business schools: it offers the chance to begin, revitalize, invigorate or deepen conversations about the potential for business research and their other endeavours to be impactful.

DEFINITIONS AND PURPOSE: BROADENING OUR MINDSET

To deliver sustainable outcomes through research impact, business schools should be clear about what they mean by research impact. To come to a workable definition, schools should workshop the broad concept of impact, and the more specific concept of research impact, with key stakeholders, to gain their perspectives and buy-in. This is especially crucial for academic and professional staff who will be tasked with creating, capturing and communicating impact, and supporting and providing strategic direction for research impact work. Perhaps the most frequently asked question in this domain is 'What is impact?' (prefaced above), followed by 'How do you measure it?' (discussed later in this chapter).

While we stated the definition that we followed, impact can be about a variety of things, as the AACSB standards and the UK REF and ARC already cited attest to: thought leadership, public communication and media mentions; inventions, patents and commercialization; influencing policy, practice or behaviour in different economic, political, legal, social or cultural settings. Wickert et al. name five forms of impact (scholarly, practical, societal, policy, educational) and offer advice and discussion on how scholars might 'systematically extend or enlarge their research agenda or projects to amplify their impact on the challenges societies face' (Wickert et al., 2021: 297). Business schools need to come to a shared meaning based on the available definitions within their institutional environment, and the different domains in which research impact might occur. These domains might include: classrooms through research-led teaching; in policy or practitioner settings through the adoption or application of research findings and recommendations; in the public sphere by shaping the national conversation on a topic; or in commercialization outcomes from university spinoffs, inter alia. The scope for defining business school impact is thus wide. Wharton's Social Impact Initiative, for example, covers impact investing, student experiences, research and thought partnership (Wharton, 2022). These domains animate Wharton's impact vision statement as follows: 'We are inspired by the vision of business and capital markets working together to create sustainable solutions to the world's greatest social and environmental challenges.' Some national research councils' definitions of research impact are narrower. The ARC, for instance, was explicit in its advice to Australian universities in the 2018 Engagement and Impact (EI) assessment exercise that research impact was not considered to be the same thing as publicity, nor coverage in the press or social media alone. Moreover, in restricting their definition of impact to 'the contribution that research makes to the economy, society, environment or culture, beyond the contribution to academic research' (arc.gov.au/about-arc/strategies/research-impact-principles-and-framework), the effects of the uptake of research *within universities* potentially fall outside the scope for assessment.

Why Do Business Schools Do Research, and For Whom?

To our minds, however, the guiding question for impact discussions within business schools should be less about the 'what', or even the 'how'. Instead, we suggest that conversations begin by asking '*why*' and '*for whom*'. Why are we doing (this) research? Who will use it? What benefits will it bring to those constituencies? Starting with the question of 'Why are we doing this?' is vital. It means that as researchers we are explicitly asking questions about the purpose of our work, our values and commitments, and the difference that we want it to make. To know the intended purpose makes it easier to envision the effects or benefits subsequent to use. It can also give us an answer to the 'So what?' question so often posed of academic work.

Business school mission and vision statements should capture purpose, of course, and it may well be that researchers can draw inspiration from their institution's mission statement in relation to their own work. It seems that, increasingly, business school mission statements make mention of questions of sustainability, inclusion or broader social purpose. The same should be done by individual researchers in respect of their own programmes of research/research themes, and certainly when applying for research funding in competitive or national grants scheme where this is precisely required. To give one example, the University of KwaZulu-Natal's Graduate School of Business and Leadership, South Africa, seeks to 'educate managers and leaders to create value for society.

We are a school that is academically excellent, innovative in research and critically engaged with society and its institutions'.

Stakeholder mapping at the level of the individual project as well as the business school more broadly could be beneficial (see Chapter 2). It can contribute to identifying potential and actual key external partnerships and potential/actual collaborations that foster impactful outcomes. Who are the potential or actual end users, or research users? If we cannot get to those users directly, who are the gatekeepers or influencers with whom we need to connect? The users of our research may also be considered beneficiaries; however, this latter group are not necessarily or always the direct users themselves. For example, primary school teachers may come to use a particular educational technique, or a revised educational policy, that is based on academic research. They may be the end users and accrue benefits; but the teachers' pupils may also profit from the implementation of this new technique or policy although they are not the direct users, and the researcher may never meet those pupils directly.

Sometimes the very idea of the 'end user' can seem very far off in the future for researchers, and perhaps discourage them from undertaking the work needed to achieve impact. Just as publishing in top journals can take years, so too can the generation of research impact. There may be a series of people or organizations that one needs to connect with before getting to the end user. For instance, the Australia-based training provider Research Impact Academy (https://researchimpactacademy.com/) asks its trainees to consider not only who is the end user but, crucially, who is the 'next user'. This very pithy and practical question can help to break down some of the psychological distance and anxiety surrounding impact generation. Effective industry engagement starts by asking: what are the strategic priorities and needs of the current and next end users, and with what sorts of expertise and practitioner knowledges would the research knowledge interact to produce impactful outcomes? Key skills of active listening, empathy, and problem identification ideally through co-design of research (impact) projects with external stakeholders could ensure that industry and community relevance is built into the business school research work from its conception. If this work is able to address pressing strategic issues or priorities in an organization, and a trusting relationship with that partner has been established, it is more likely that our research will be adopted into practice.

Ethics and Politics of Research Impact

Questions of 'why' and 'for whom' are political and moral questions. The research impact agenda thus underscores the value-laden nature of our research ambitions, and the politics of the institutional environment for research and research funding in different settings. At the time of writing (2022, prior to the national election), there are concerns in Australia about political interference by the government in national research funding priorities and awards. The same applies in other countries. The current focus on enhancing commercial outcomes from publicly funded research appears to overshadow non-commercial outcomes. This is affecting the research of academics based in arts, humanities or social science disciplines, whose research knowledge might not lend itself so readily to commodification, or to those doing basic (rather than applied) research.

Dr Alison Barnes of the Australian NTEU (National Tertiary Education Union) wrote that Australian Prime Minister Scott Morrison's 2022 announcement of $1.6 billion in funds for manufacturing research 'was a slap in the face to talented academics across Australia, who perform vital work for the public good' (Barnes, 2022: 2). She expressed her concern that 'only research that aligns with its [the Coalition govern-ment's] own priorities will be supported'. She continued that: 'The fine print in the plan is shocking. Institutions are being told they must rearrange their pay and promotion arrangements to favour commercially oriented researchers or they could miss out on research funding' (Barnes, 2022: 2). In this context, it might seem that patents, inventions and commercial impacts are valued more greatly than other types of potential impact in assessments of national research grant proposals.

Nested within or at least alongside such political concerns are moral ones that impinge upon questions of purpose. Are the researchers willing to accept funding from defence or military organizations, cigarette man-ufacturers, or financial institutions that invest superannuation funds into fossil fuel stocks? Do they consider the impacts of these social actors negative for society? If so, do they want to avoid them, or work alongside them to co-create change? Or do they become part of the 'problem'? And what is it feasible to expect in terms of the scale and substance of any prospective change? In the business school institutional environment, the Responsible Research in Business and Management Network (RRBM; https://www.rrbm.network/) puts public/social good concerns front and centre of its advocacy and support efforts (see also the Impact and

Sustainable Finance Faculty Consortium;https://www.impactandsustaina blefinance.org/index.html). RRBM is a virtual organization created by a small number of scholars from 23 university-based business schools in ten countries. It gives a 'vision of business schools and scholars world-wide having successfully transformed their research toward responsible science, producing credible knowledge that is ultimately useful for addressing problems important to business and society'. Supported by accrediting bodies, including the AACSB and the European Foundation for Management Development (EFMD), and the GRLI and UN PRME, RRBM's seven principles comprise: Service to Society; Valuing Both Basic and Applied Contributions; Valuing Plurality and Multidisciplinary Collaboration; Sound Methodology; Stakeholder Involvement; Impact on Stakeholders; and Broad Dissemination. Its website offers an excellent one-stop-shop for examples of best practice, resources/position papers, and promotion of conferences, special issues and expertise in responsible management. National associations of business schools have showcased the societal impact of members' research to demonstrate the value, and values, of their work to stakeholders. The UK-based CABS, for instance, produced a report on 'The Impact of Business School Research' (https:// charteredabs.org/impact-business-school-research-published-today-abs -support-call-rebalance-research-fundi/). The report's broad aim is to 'rebalance research funding'; that is to say, to ensure that business and management researchers gain a greater share of available research funds in the UK. The report features impact case studies of different industry settings, sectors and types of work/occupations including the automotive industry, social enterprise, defence, green energy, SMEs and employ-ment relations.

A focus on creating a shared understanding of research impact, and addressing questions of purpose, requires a broadening of the mindset of business schools and researchers about research. It requires asking why, as well as what and how, and to plan for impacts purposefully from the outset of our work. It underscores that traditional research outputs like journal articles are but one potentially valuable output from research, and that researchers and their schools need to work together to translate their work and create pathways to impact through dissemination and research communications, industry engagement and project co-design, or commercialization.

CREATING AND CAPTURING IMPACT FROM RESEARCH PROJECTS

From answering questions of purpose, business schools might then turn to these:

1. The question of *how* research impact is generated or created, often framed in the language of research translation and the activities/ outputs from research that are used to build a pathway to impact.
2. The question of *what* is measured, documented and evidenced. Impact is the demonstrable effect or change resulting from the use/ adoption of research knowledge, and is evidenced through sources such as testimonials of users/beneficiaries or other third-party data (for example, organizational reports).

In impact lingo, these two questions are about creating and capturing research impact.

Dissemination Models and Thought Leadership

Disseminating research knowledge through the media, public or outreach events, workshops, or other forms of civic engagement may be considered the basis for impact depending on the definition or framework the researcher is using. It is critical here to be clear on the definition of impact. AACSB Standard 8 on the impact of scholarship would cover thought leadership activities not only within academic fields but also in the public realm. Examples of activities may include business school webinar series, high-profile lectures, publications in *The Conversation* or industry and practitioner magazines, or keynote addresses at industry conferences (Fisher, 2020). These activities serve to raise awareness or present important or new insights or understandings about a pressing social issue. Their importance is underlined in the Australian context, where the Australian Business Deans Council (ABDC) is promoting a book that aims to improve how business researchers communicate their research. The book is titled: *Tell Us: What Are You Doing? Improving How you Communicate your Academic Research, Relevance and Expertise* (Falkner-Rose, 2022). It covers topics including understanding the media and working with journalists, building your profile, developing your strategy and content, and connecting with social media. This public-facing work is vital in the domain of sustainability and specifically climate change where a key challenge is framing public understandings so as to generate behaviour change amongst organizations, consumers, the general public and politicians.

Altmetric (2017) provided the following recommendations for attracting attention to one's work:

- Write a lay summary of your research and introduce it in relevant lists and online forums.
- Upload and make available data, images, posters and other files via a platform share.
- Start your own blog (or contribute to an existing one).
- Reach out to key bloggers about your work, and look at Altmetric's details pages for other articles in your discipline (discussed below).
- Include a link to your work in your email signature or online profile.
- Work with the press office at your publisher or institution.
- Share links to your work via Twitter and other social media after presenting at conferences.
- Register for an ORCID ID so others can easily discover your work.
- Make your work available via Open Access.

To make it easy for others to cite your research – especially if it is in a non-journal-paper format – researchers should include a preferred citation (with all the relevant bibliographic information) that others can copy and paste into their documents. To find out who might be citing and potentially using your research outputs, Altmetric tools can be useful. Altmetric tools (for example, Altmetric.com, which institutions can subscribe to and use its Altmetric explorer; or Elsevier PlumAnalytics) can be beneficial, for instance, if you are looking to track mentions of your research in policy settings. To make sure Altmetric identifies mentions of your academic research, Altmetric (2017) also recommends the following:

- Always link to a page that includes your research's unique identifier (for example, DOI, PubMedID), such as the publisher's or institutional repository abstract page.
- The link needs to be in the main body of the text, as Altmetric does not identify links included in headers or other sections of the page.
- Altmetric needs to be tracking the source that has mentioned the work.

Altmetric data are used by the *Financial Times* in their rankings of universities' societal impact of teaching, research and operations (Jack, 2020). Jack (2022) reported on how rankings providers are considering how best to tackle the measurement of societal impact as 'schools scramble to embrace sustainability'. Jack (2022) cites the Rotterdam School of Management (RSM), which has created a measure of the societal impact of research outputs. RSM's policy director has 'studied the proportion of papers published by academics in top schools between 2018 and 2021 that addressed topics in the UN's Sustainable Development Goals'. This analysis noted the impressive performances on this metric of Edinburgh, Melbourne and Esade.

The problem with dissemination models implicit in the examples above, however, is that any effects that may ensue from such communications efforts (for example, changing awareness, knowledge or opinions) are very difficult to capture (Watson, 2003) and attribute to one's research. Scholars may be able to gather data about the reach of their research – the numbers of readers, stakeholders, users, downloaders, beneficiaries, and the profile of those constituencies. But they do not necessarily get information on the significance of their work, and this is because these 'push' communication activities offer little insight into the *use* to which our work is subsequently put, and therefore the difference it makes. Dissemination-only strategies for impact hold limited control for researchers, meaning that our research findings might be used in ways and to ends that we did not intend, perhaps even generating negative impacts. Engagement-based models offer better potential for understanding impact in context.

Engagement Models: Translation as the Pathway to Impact

Engagement-based models that involve multiple and multi-directional communications, especially through collaborations with external partners, offer another avenue for impact generation (Dodson, 2015). Undertaking partnerships and ideally co-designing research with partners is very much aligned with the ethos and requirements of SDG 17. This SDG states that '[a] successful development agenda requires inclusive partnerships – at the global, regional, national and local levels – built upon principles and values, and upon a shared vision and shared goals placing people and the planet at the centre' (https://www.un.org/sustainabledevelopment/ globalpartnerships/). In our view, co-production and engagement-based models offer potentially greater control over the use of research, and thus a greater potential to better understand and evidence claims for research impact. This is the model for impact favoured by the ARC, who define research engagement as 'the *interaction* between researchers and research end-users outside of academia, for the *mutually beneficial transfer* of knowledge, technologies, methods and resources' (emphasis added, https://dataportal.arc.gov.au/ei/nationalreport/2018/pages/introduction/index.html?id=definitions#:~:text=Research%20engagement%20is%20the%20interaction,%2C%20technologies%2C%20methods%20or%20resources). Leading business schools will have structures specifically designed to enable and support the development of industry partnerships and researcher–end-user interactions. At Ivey Business School, for example, Professor Tima Bansal is the founder of 'Innovation North' (https://innovationnorth.ca/), which specifically brings together business leaders and researchers to collaborate, and to co-create innovation through the application of the systems thinking required for sustainable development. She also founded the Network for Business Sustainability, with the goal to share evidence-based sustainable guidance for leaders (https://nbs.net/), and Ivey's Centre for Building Sustainable Value, which seeks to empower leaders to 'transform business in a world where sustainability is fundamental to organizational success and societal prosperity' (https://www.ivey.uwo.ca/sustainability/).

Research translation – 'the synthesis, exchange and application of knowledge by relevant stakeholders' (World Health Organization, 2005) – is at the heart of engagement and should ideally be planned from the project outset, and ideally with users. Of course, this is not always feasible. Translation is the pathway to impact, and a social and relational set of processes subject to the vagaries of time, people and context. Given that it involves people and organizations, research translation will not necessarily be linear, completely predictable or wholly successful, and it will likely be a time-consuming, yet potentially highly rewarding process (Oliver and Cairney, 2019). One noted challenge with this work is that people leave organizations, and so established contacts and gatekeepers who provide legitimacy and resources for research impact may come and go. Multiple interactions over time between researchers and research users become the practices through which research translation occurs. Given the number and diversity of research users with whom business schools may work, it is barely surprising that pathways to impact are unique, and no 'standard model' exists. As evidence, a report prepared by a team from King's College London and Digital Science (2015) explored the nature, scale and beneficiaries recorded in the 6,975 impact cases submitted to the 2014 UK REF. The authors stated that 'the most striking observation to be made is the 3,709 unique different ways that the research to impact pathway takes' (King's College London and Digital Science, 2015: 38).

Translation is a practical activity that involves creating, or ideally co-creating with partners, outputs and activities from academic research. The idea is to communicate in terms as accessible as possible the outcomes and significance of our research, to what end and how they can be applied or used by stakeholders. Outputs here are not only traditional research articles, but practitioner pieces, reports, press releases, PowerPoint slide decks, short videos, standards, recommendations for health guidance, infographics, podcasts, conference presentations, exhibitions, community seminars, briefings, workshops, manager training, patents or licences, and so on – a myriad of different verbal and visual communications and rhetorical strategies for creating understanding of business schools' research, and how and why it should be used. To use some of the lingo, it would make the research 'actionable'. This is importance because impact, from our perspective, is something that is generated by users of our research.

Measuring and Evidencing Impact: Some Positive Examples

If we want to find out whether impact has occurred, and to document and evidence it, researchers need to ask their users and beneficiaries. Impact is also about demonstrable/provable, measurable or discernible *change*, linked to the use of our research, and may be represented with quantitative or qualitative indicators. The implication of both these points is that the particular measures, or metrics, used to indicate the change or effect that has occurred following use, adoption or adaptation of our translated research will depend on the project. These indicators can take the form of increases in particular variables such as jobs, income, health or well-being, or decreases in variables such as stress, occupational injuries or costs. Importantly, no change can be an important impact in some contexts. For example, if the researchers' goal is to contribute to the preservation of some aspect of the natural environment, or to halt the disappearance of certain languages (for example, Indigenous languages), then retaining the status quo (that is, no change) is impact. Conducting investigations into the impact of the work is akin to conducting 'research on our research', with impact a kind of 'dependent variable'. It is vital that researchers keep documentation that demonstrates or proves the existence of these indicators of change, or user benefits. This evidence is vital in underpinning research impact cases. Testimonies from organizational stakeholders such as chief executive officers or chief human resource officers are common forms of evidence used for impact case studies. Evidence of citation, or use of research, may also be found in an organization's minutes or agenda for C-suite meetings or conferences, or they may appear in policy documents or parliamentary records. A key piece of advice here is that researchers need to become good documenters of their engagement and impact work – so they need to keep all emails, ask for letters or testimonies, and archive these carefully.

The King's College London and Digital Science (2015) report on the 2014 UK REF impact case studies found that for the business and management unit of assessment (UoA), the most commonly demonstrated impacts were in these domains: informing government policy, and parliamentary scrutiny; business and industry impacts; regional innovation and enterprise; banking, finance and monetary policy; community and local government; and work, labour and employment. Other impacts related to technology commercialization, international development, health care services, and schools and education. Examples of impact cases can increasingly be found on business school websites, as part of showcasing their work to external audiences, and some of these cases are linked to sustainability. Imperial Business School, for instance, has conducted impactful sustainability-related work on Tanzanian farmers, and planning for a low-emissions future. The University of Edinburgh Business School has published work titled 'Calling time on green-washing', and the University of Technology Sydney Business School in its 2021 research report describes its 'knowledge with impact' through cases of Australian sustainable finance roadmaps, and helping business to understand and respect Indigenous rights.

Alternatively, readers can go to impact case repositories, including those from the UK REF (https://impact.ref.ac.uk/casestudies/), the ABDC (https://abdc.edu.au/) or Research Impact Canada (https://researchimpact.ca/). The UK REF has a case study database of all submitted cases to the 2014 exercise, 942 of which featured 'sustainable' in their titles. And of the 411 cases submitted in the business and management studies, several had sustainability outcomes and impacts. Examples linked to environmental sustainability (for example, work at London Metropolitan University on transport for sustainable urban environments; University of Exeter on sustainable procurement in the public and practice sectors; Heriot-Watt University on the decarbonization of freight transport; Sheffield University on low carbon supply chain resource modelling), and social and economic sustainability (for example, work at the University of Leicester on effective labour rights through international framework agreements; the University of Ulster on advancing HR practice through employee well-being strategies; Edinburgh Napier University on improved employment outcomes for disadvantaged groups by informing policy; and Royal Holloway embedding sustainability into management decision-making).

ORGANIZING CAPACITY AND LIFTING CAPABILITY FOR IMPACT

The creation and capture of research impact require institutional strategy, structure and support. Where the research impact agenda is 'new', or still emerging, key tasks involve building institutional and researcher literacy about impact (Bayley and Phipps, 2017), lifting capability for academic staff (likely not all, but some) to do this work, and organizing capacity and support for academic and professional staff to do it (Bayley et al., 2017). A crucial part of the puzzle is to devise appropriate incentives and rewards to do work that is potentially time-consuming, sometimes years-long, and hard work. Recognizing and showcasing achievements through institutional communication channels including websites, reports, industry events, podcasts, and award ceremonies is important to motivate and reward. For many staff, though, the motivation is intrinsic and about the meaning and experience of making a substantive difference to sustainable outcomes.

Developing a Research Impact Strategy and Ethos

Some universities and/or business schools have strategies in place (for example, La Trobe University in Australia). Schools would need to dovetail with their university's plans, but where none exists, or the school is independent of a university, the AACSB has a useful document titled 'Research that matters: An action plan for creating business school research that positively impacts society' (published with Sage Publishing) in which it identifies three key components of research that can shape schools' capacity to have positive societal impact. These are that the research is '*cross-disciplinary*, *intersectional* [at the intersection of academia and practice], and *actionable* [i.e., that creates real change]' (AACSB, 2021b; emphasis added). The thought paper gives a roadmap for schools to follow based on these components, which can be used to generate an action plan. The six-step action plan involves these tasks:

1. Consider your mission.
2. Identify specific areas of focus for your school. The report cites The Boston University Questrom School of Business which has created an institute-based structure focused on five strategic focus areas for its impact work, including social impact (to cover sustainable finance, green bonds, impact investing, corporate social responsibility (CSR), behaviour change for the good, and sustainability).
3. Leverage existing frameworks (for example, SDGs, GRI UN Global Compact, ESG). The report cites Rotterdam School of Management at Erasmus University which evaluates its faculty publications in terms of their relevance to the SDGs (as noted earlier) and produces videos that 'provide tangible examples of how management knowledge can contribute to the SDGs'. (AACSB, 2021b: 13)
4. Create a micro-strategic plan for societal impact.
5. Cultivate relationships with appropriate stakeholders.
6. Champion your research cause.

Business schools thus need an explicit approach to planning, creating, capturing and communicating their research impact. Clear action plans on impact, with key performance indicators, incentive and reward mechanisms, need to be informed by the broader mission and strategic and operational context of the school. Rickards et al. (2020) highlight that research impact should become an 'ethos' within universities, by which they mean a 'co-created, embedded and positive research impact culture' (2020: 3). One example of research impact strategy building comes from Monash Business School, Australia. It spent two years building its strategy, structure and plan in these respects. The process involved focus groups with heads of department, researchers and directors of research, who then created suggestions for a four-point strategy. An Associate Dean Research Impact (ADRI) was then appointed to develop and deliver the strategy. A Faculty Research Impact Sub-committee (with quarterly meetings) was established, chaired by the ADRI, with representation from all departments and research centres within the business school. These representatives act as local impact champions within their areas, bringing examples of impactful work to the committee, whilst disseminating information downwards. Mandatory research impact training was given to the committee members by an external training provider (RIA;

the Research Impact Academy); and then voluntary impact training was (and still is) offered to all academic and professional staff within the business school. At the time of writing, nearly 200 staff have received this training through RIA. The business school also established a grants scheme – the Impact Acceleration Grants Scheme – with cash and in-kind support for 12-month impact projects. These grants can be used to create and capture future research impact, or to go back to completed projects and attend to identifying, documenting and evidencing historical impacts. Following completion of the grants, awardees are offered the opportunity to have videos professionally produced about the impacts they have generated, and 1,200-word narrative pieces written for them (with their input) by a journalist. Monash Business School is also consulting staff in regard to a proposed performance framework which makes research impact a pathway for staff's career development.

Impact Through Cross-Disciplinary Research

Cross-disciplinary research can enhance the potential impact of business schools' research, as the AACSB advises, especially when business school academics work in larger multidisciplinary teams outside their faculty. On one hand, business school scholars can provide expertise in the kinds of processes that pathways to impact may involve, such as commercialization, or organizational change. On the other hand, business schools can bring substantive expertise to address wicked problems like climate change or other sustainability concerns which demand multiple perspectives. Examples from the AACSB report mentioned previously include Maastricht University's School of Business and Economics' Service Robots in Healthcare and Hospitality team. Working with business, healthcare, design and robotics colleagues, the team received EU funding to explore how service robots can address societal challenges including loneliness, an ageing population and staff shortages. The team produced evidence-based recommendations and typologies for industry partners. A commercialization example from Rowan University involves their Rohrer College of Business's Studio 231, a cross-disciplinary learning laboratory and makerspace for students and staff from business and engineering and from arts, including anthropology. The projects created in this space have included the development of pet prosthetics and drone software for autonomous flights to aid first responders in crisis situations (AACSB, 2021b: 8).

Brown, Deletic and Wong (2015) give a personal account of the challenges and positive outcomes from building a large cross-disciplinary collaboration between social and biophysical scientists in a multi-site, high-value water management project. They describe the tensions across paradigms and working practices, and offer five principles to 'help academics to overcome these biases' (Brown et al., 2015: 316):

1. Forge a shared mission, 'sufficiently broad to incorporate meaningful roles for all disciplinary researchers involved' (2015: 316).
2. Build 'T-shaped' researchers (those that can work within their disciplines, out into others, and back).
3. Nurture constructive dialogue via the creation of informal rules, such as interact in plain English, foster empathy and respect for different disciplinary norms, reflective practice on what works.
4. Give institutional support via clear academic career pathways for interdisciplinary work manifest in university policies, promotion criteria and seed-funding programmes.
5. Bridge research, policy and practice, for example through involvement of industry partners in research programme design, and critical discussions of approach and results. Brown et al. also address how particular stakeholders in the research environment of universities, including funders, institutions, publishers and researchers themselves, can promote interdisciplinary research.

Enablers

A final crucial piece of the puzzle consists of the multiple enablers of a research impact strategy. Library staff play a crucial role in enabling distribution and tracking the citation, and potential use, of academic research through Altmetric training and customized searches. The AACSB's (2021b) thought paper on research impact action plans, mentioned previously, noted that business library staff at the Foster School of Business, University of Washington, work to identify engagement opportunities for staff, including events to promote grand challenges research, additions to the library collection on these topics, and open-access publishing. Research office staff who support committee work, administer grant schemes, support and advise researchers on pathways to impact, and collect and work on evidencing impact cases are vital service providers. Many universities and business schools, such as Warwick Business School, now have dedicated research impact directors and officers. Marketing communication staff, or external professional writers, can help to develop case narratives and promote and showcase staff work. IT staff can help with systems for capturing and documenting engagement and impact activities, including the Pure system, which has an Impact Module that allows researchers to archive their impact documents whilst linking to engagement activities, and validated research outputs and funding associated with it. Private providers of impact services can provide not only case writing, but also impact training, and software packages for tracking and document impact (for example, Vertigo Ventures). Publishers are now commissioning research impact workbooks, and other publishing on this topic. Examples include Emerald Publishing, which has developed, with co-authors Bayley and Phipps (2020), research impact literacy workbooks for institutions and individual researchers to use.

CONCLUSION

This chapter has pursued the view that the creation, capture and communication of research impact by business schools and their researchers is a vital avenue for achieving sustainability goals. But there is work to be done within business schools to raise awareness, and to develop knowledge, capability, literacy and disposition to undertake this often time-consuming, yet highly rewarding work. The chapter has underscored the importance of understanding why we research the topics we do, and being explicit about the changes we wish to see happen as a result of our research being used or adopted. While not underestimating the importance of thought leadership and dissemination approaches to impact, the chapter recommends engagement-driven or co-production models to enhance the chances of research impact generation. Building the impact literacy of future researchers and business school leaders is critical task, and one on which much sustainability work rests.

5. Accreditations, rankings and business school governance

To make the sustainability agenda happen in reality, business schools cannot simply keep going as they have done over the years. They have to change their 'business as usual' and do so in a meaningful way. The previous chapters delved into stakeholders, teaching and learning, as well as research impact issues that need to be addressed to embed the SDGs in schools' research and educational agendas. In this chapter we take a strategic and operational perspective on the actions that are necessary to transform business schools' modus operandi. In so doing, we will rejoin some of our earlier arguments.

One thing you can almost guarantee when you meet a business school dean or representative is that they will boast about the accreditations their school holds or how well they do on a range of rankings. Such discussions are commonplace, with schools waxing lyrical about their position or accreditation badges. Rankings and accreditations are explicit mechanisms for business schools to signal their position in the market. They are considered to be a source of competitive advantage (Thomas et al., 2014). Accreditations and rankings are perceived to signal 'quality' programmes and prestige (Tullis and Camey, 2007). They are a signifier of value. They not only help to establish a reputation for quality, but they also give international exposure (Thomas et al., 2014). Worldwide, the AACSB lists about 900 business schools and the *Financial Times* lists 100 MBAs. Business schools that hold the triple accreditation crown perceive themselves to be part of the elite group of business schools, and they laud their premium position, be it in terms of research, education or societal impact. A school that holds the triple crown is a school that holds at the same time the main three accreditations: AACSB, EQUIS and AMBA. There were about 110 business schools worldwide that had such standing in 2021. This constitutes roughly 1 per cent of the total number of business schools (MBA Today, 2022). For instance, there were 23 in the UK, 11 in China, 4 in Germany and 3 in Australia. These accreditation bodies actively influence business schools in all their activities. They influence their academic faculty and staff recruitment, as well as their educational offering and their governance (Dameron and Durand, 2009; Mottis, 2008). The AACSB's main focus is on the curriculum and learning outcomes, whereas EQUIS's main focus is on continuous improvement, comparisons between schools and internationalization.

The importance that business schools bestow on accreditations highlights their role in influencing their adoption and genuine adherence to the SDGs. As mentioned in the introductory chapter, accrediting bodies are incorporating the SDGs in their accreditation standards, but for many business schools, this has had little impact on their operations. In many instances, this has been limited to changing the wording of their mission and vision statements so that they can declare that they embrace the SDGs. However, many are still paying lip service to them in their educational offering, their operations and governance. Sustainability is often conceived as a 'topic', rather than a mindset, a new consciousness that requires business schools to radically transform (Kurucz et al., 2014).

This may be one of the reasons why the AACSB has established new standards with a new focus on engagement and societal impact and will assess how business schools perform in this regard. EQUIS also clearly signals that the PRME should be embedded in business school policies and operations, teaching and research, and it is one of the criteria for accreditation (EFMD, 2022). One can surmise that unless there are visible cases where business schools fail to get the accreditation because they did not embed the SDGs, or maybe, more powerfully, one school loses accreditation because of not doing so, the true adoption of the SDGs may be slower than expected. Accreditations are a force for change not only, as just mentioned, because business schools want to have the 'badge' to be recognized as quality players, but also because they foster competitive mimicry (Thomas et al., 2014). Due to their desire to be accredited, business schools converge and they become more homogenized; and hence if the accreditation bodies make a strong stance about the SDGs and about thoroughly assessing the extent to which they are embedded in business schools, it is most likely that, one by one, business schools would take up the SDGs. They will all follow suit in their quest to be seen as global players, providing prestigious education and attracting the best students and staff from around the world, leading to them to maintain or increase their revenues.

The same argument can be made regarding rankings, notably the most prestigious ones such as the FT, THE or QS World University Rankings. These rankings used traditional measures, such as Graduate Management

Admissions Test (GMAT®) scores, salaries or employment outlook, but they have yet to assess the espousal of the SDGs, such as socially relevant research or access to gaining knowledge, skills and opportunities needed to address the SDGs. If they did, maybe there would also be more enthusiasm for delivering on the SDGs: 'What gets measured gets managed. If the rankings were to evaluate the societal value of research, schools would start managing those metrics' (Berry et al., 2021). While there is no doubt that accreditations and rankings influence what gets measured in business schools, one can start questioning who wags the tail? Business school deans and other bodies such as national research assessment regimes such as REF (UK) or ERA (Australia) have to change so that the SDGs are truly pursued, rather than merely given lip service (for instance by limiting their efforts to having a sustainability lead or an engagement and impact associate dean). As Weybrecht (2022) wrote:

> Too many institutions are not living up to their own green rhetoric … while schools acknowledge the SDGs, their leaders are not fundamentally changing the way they operate. This includes the processes, incentives and training that influence daily behaviour. There is no coherent strategy, and any specific guidelines are often separate from a school's overarching objectives and mission.

They can make things happen by changing how they govern the schools, allocate resources, and notably by changing the recruitment standards and the rewards systems in use.

RECRUITMENT AND REWARDS

'Academic focus limits business schools' contribution to society', and there is much criticism that a large part of business schools' academic research concentrates on 'abstract, abstruse and overly academic topics with little resonance beyond the higher education sector' (Financial Times, 2022). While, of course, one cannot generalize, in business schools, especially those that are accredited, the main assessment criterion for recruitment of academics is the number of top-tier publications. Often the number of recent top-tier publications, so that they can be counted in the various rankings or research assessments, is the most salient criterion. Such publications are largely about 'theoretical contributions' and encourage focus and depth in a specific field, rather than application and the examination of environmentally or socially relevant phenomena. This means that scholars, notably junior scholars, have little incentive to engage in sustainability-oriented research or develop inter-disciplinary and transdisciplinary collaborations that may facilitate the tackling of sustainability issues. Tourish (2020) argues that this is a crisis. While he talks precisely about the management discipline, this applies to all business school areas of scholarship: 'We neglect really important issues in favour of bite-sized chunks of research that are more likely to find quick publication in leading journals' (Tourish, 2020: 99). Writing readable (sic!) papers that are stimulating, engender curiosity, and mean-ingful and impactful is not of concern. What matters is to play the game and, more often than not, it means writing formulaic, dull papers that purportedly develop theory that will be published in the leading journals. This has led to the common view that the only things that matter are the publications. What matters are 'the prints that can be counted' and not what the publication is about, its message and impact. The academic research content is primary, and practitioners or policy implications are second thoughts, or non-existent. Recruitment standards and research incentives are in line with the recruitment process; top-tier publications get rewarded. Academics that do not comply and, for instance, are interested in publishing in practitioners' journals, or writing books, do suffer the consequences. They might see their career stall or, at worst, find themselves being 'performance managed' out of their role or given demanding teaching loads, meaning that they have no time to do anything but teach. The other consequence of overteaching is that the quality of teaching also suffers, as staff have little time to prepare or refresh their materials. This means that they cannot carry out sustainability-oriented research, nor can they necessarily create appropriate syllabi or engage in the interdisciplinary educational activities needed to develop new programmes.

Stremersch et al. (2022), ironically writing in one top-tier journal, reflected adamantly about the current situation and studied the problems with current business schools' research. They concluded, amongst other things, that it had little societal benefit. They clearly pointed the finger at the research metrics and research incentives as one of the reasons why, and argued that relevance to non-academic audiences needs to be incorporated in research matrices. Business schools have emphasized academic rigour (with the proxy measurement being top-tier publications) to the detriment of any practical and impactful research. The same sentiment is shared by Aguinis et al. (2020: 135):

> The increased pressure to publish in 'A' journals means the new bottom line for valuing academic research is 'an A is an A.' Faculty recruiting committees and promotion and tenure panels readily discuss how many A's a candidate has published and how many A's are needed for a favourable decision, while conversations about the distinctive intellectual value of a publication are often secondary to its categorical membership in journals.

Narrow-minded recruitment and incentive criteria, where journals' rankings are a proxy for the value of a publication, will restrict progress towards developing an academic faculty that is sustainability and impact-oriented in their research and their teaching. Without creating a culture that steers these recruits away from concentrating on narrowly focused topics and theoretical contributions written specifically for top-tier journals and where rewarding staff is solely on a very limited range of publications in specific outlets means that it is unlikely that there will be a shift in mindset.

One can surmise that if schools started counting research outputs that addressed issues related to the SDGs, things could change. For instance, these outputs could include traditional theory-driven articles on sustainability that push our understanding on how and why the sustainability agenda can be pursued, what it means and why it may be dismissed. These outputs may also be translation articles or practically relevant articles that can be used in the classrooms, and can guide students and managers in executive education on how to drive the sustainability agenda. They could also include books or chapters that students actually read, and even enjoy reading, because they enliven sustainability issues and are often more approachable to read. They could also do so by rewarding education articles that report on service learning or internship in sustainability-oriented organizations such as renewable energy companies, or organizations fighting child exploitation, or refugee centres. This also leads us to highlight that the paradigm that only research matters, and that teaching is a load, aka a punishment for poor researcher, has to change. A balanced approach is necessary. To genuinely be a beacon of sustainability, business schools cannot discard teaching. 'Developing the moral compass of students' (Thompson, 2010) is critical and should be foremost in business schools' agendas. Business schools should reward scholars who contribute to both research and teaching equally (Aguinis et al., 2020).

CHANGING THE RULES OF THE BUSINESS SCHOOLS' GAME

Our exposition so far implies that to embed the SDGs, business school deans should change their strategic decision-making and their current modus operandi. This means that, as Thomas and Ambrosini (2021) explain, they aim to break free from the current institutional field (Oliver, 1991) and transform it. If they do not so, the present situation, epitomized by the 'publish or perish' ethos and dominance of external rankings, will remain. A paradigm shift is necessary, but given the commitment to the old paradigm and the perceived cost of making this shift, it is unlikely to be easy, even if there is willingness (Van der Brugge and Van Raak, 2007). This is currently a big if, with some in charge being regularly described as dinosaurs, refusing to accept that the world is changing. Arguably, they suffer from 'strategic myopia' and this leads to organizational inertia (Tripsas and Gavetti, 2000). These leaders cannot see the world differently and remain in the same frame. They believe that, regardless of what the world around them tells them about the importance of impact on society or being engaged with stakeholders and publishing meaningful work, the rules of the game will not change and that 'counting the A publication' is all that matters. They cannot adapt and cannot even see the need to change, as they are so entrenched in their beliefs (Barr et al., 1992). They simply do not get that

> we must accept that we're in a race against time to avert a climate catastrophe that poses an existential threat to humanity. We urgently need to start living within our planetary boundaries, before we reach irreversible tipping points that do permanent damage to our biodiversity and critical ecosystems – nature's guarantors of happy, healthy and prosperous societies. (Paul Polman, cited in CABS, 2021c: 2)

They may also find it difficult that millennials, who make up a large proportion of the current student body, have broader concerns than other generations. Of course, they have economic concerns, but they also have social, ethical and ecological values (Cheng, 2019). If this denial of climate crisis is limited to a few, this is possibly not an irreversible problem, but if the majority of the business schools' leaders do not recognize the need for change, then nothing will happen (Almeida and Melo, 2017).

The transition towards embedding the SDGs in all aspects of business schools' 'life' will require lots of efforts, breaking paradigms and creating new ones, as well as taking new actions and developing new structures, systems and processes. The current operating 'business as usual' culture and the values people hold need to change (Bertassini et al., 2021). Without getting into the change management literature, one knows that for any organization to change, they need to know why they should change, what to change into and how to do so. Here we know the why, this is an imperative and we have discussed the drivers throughout the chapters. What to change into relates to business schools becoming institutions that embrace principles of responsible business education and embed the SDGs in their ways of doing things, and at all levels and in all areas of operation. As just explained, we hope that the 'why' will become accepted, and that leaders will commit to changing the mindset that underpins the values needed to influence a change in behaviour (Bertassini et al., 2021). This transformation is a journey. It is about continuous improvement, as most deep change is, and it cannot happen overnight.

There is no doubt that the 'how' is not straightforward. It involves breaking away from path dependencies, the way we used to think and do things, and removing dysfunctional values and processes (Suddaby et al., 2020). It means that breaking free from the field and radically reconfiguring it; it cannot be down to a few deans. It has to be a broad and an in-depth effort. It has to involve many of the field's stakeholders, including those that are at the institutional level, business school strategic level, or members of staff. The transition-to-sustainability literature (see, for instance, reviews by Bertassini et al. 2021 or Savaget et al., 2019) highlights that to make the move to being a sustainability organization, an organization needs to change its behaviours, but this may be confusing and people at all levels may resist change. And, as just mentioned, change does not happen in silos. The entire ecosystem in which an organization operates, both its internal and external environment, needs to be in sync and create a self-reinforcing cycle for transitioning to the embeddedness of the SDGs.

This field of stakeholders includes the journal ranking list bodies (which prioritize theoretically based and discipline-based 'top-tier' journals). Such lists include the University of Texas at Dallas (UTD), CABS (UK) or the ABDC (Australia) lists. These lists are used to inform the recruitment and incentive criteria we have just talked about. The national research assessments – for example, REF (UK) or ERA (Australia) – that are linked to research funding and also rank business schools are aligned to these lists and also demand publications in top-tier academic journals, rendering impact and social relevance secondary considerations (recognizing that some of these concerns/topics may indeed be published in top tier publications). Why are these bodies not following suit and committing to help business schools tackle sustainability issues and foster their achievement of the SDGs?

We also have to recognize that the other important stakeholders who need to shift mindset are academics themselves. Dialogue between stakeholders and developing new values that will be taken for granted are critical to making things happen. Change has to be driven both bottom up and top down. Deans can impose as much as they want but if staff are not committed themselves, the transformation will be stalled:

> For many faculty, the main focus of their existence is the search for the holy grail of publishing in A* journals. This has become a major industry in its own right ... We are complicit in creating a publishing system that serves our purposes but has very little value beyond that except for the journal publishers and for the minority who publish at the highest leve. (Thomas and Starkey, 2019)

Tourish (2020) makes a similar point. He blames academics (this said, can we blame junior people who need a position, or anyone who cannot take the risk of losing their job?) who, as mentioned earlier, are interested in 'bite-sized chunks of research' to get top publications. Thomas and Ambrosini (2021) also include heads of departments, who worry about their reputation and condone the research rankings' obsession, as well as editors and reviewers who, by and large, pay scant attention to application and relevance to society and the SDGs (recognizing there are exceptions with some top journals being about impact, such as the *Academy of Management Perspectives*, or sustainability, like *Business Strategy and the Environment*, or encourage debate about business schools such as the *Academy of Management Learning and Education*). They also include the aforementioned academic funding bodies that hardly ever reward interdisciplinary management research. Recruiting new staff who embrace sustainability values and can demonstrate their meaningfulness might be a way to start shifting the mindset of the old guard, who actually may not have had the chance to understand the need for change, because the business schools operate in their old systems, notably reward and incentives structures. We are almost back to the old saying that structure leads performance, and culture eats strategy for breakfast!

SOME PROMISING CHANGES

Some would argue that the situation is not that gloomy, as there are some breakthroughs. We fully agree that there is a wealth of examples, but we are arguing that they are still lauded as being exceptional rather than the norm. The institutional field will have genuinely changed when it is taken for granted that the SDGs are part of every business schools' teaching, research, engagement activities and operations. There are a range of promising and inspiring examples and some noticeable changes, but few, if any, business schools address all aspects of their operations, and the transformation of the institutional field players is patchy.

On this institutional front, some of the key institutional players, the AACSB and EQUIS, are starting to assess, to some extent, impact, engagement and the adherence to and promotion of the SDGs. They stress that sustainability should be embedded in business schools' operations. While not being explicit about sustainability, some national research assessments may be paving the way towards assessing this adherence by now having impact rankings (for example, ERA), and the THE Impact Rankings assess universities against the SDGs. This may mean that: 'In practice, … we are talking more to those who use and consume our research and that our focus has to be on change for the good' (Cassell, 2020: 234). This indicates, as highlighted in Chapter 4, business schools have lots of leeway to make things change, and many institutional players support them. Here, the most difficult part is to change the mindset of those people who refuse change and do not see beyond the old rules, as we discussed earlier. Deans need to have a strong will and get bottom-up action so that there is enough pressure on the operational stakeholders (notably, associate deans or departmental chairs) to change current practices and monitor the implementation of these practices. Deans also need to make sure that they allocate the necessary resources and prioritize SDG initiatives in their budget. They also need to think long term, given that many deans have three- to five-year contracts, which means that newly hired deans need to come holding sustainability-oriented values.

On the teaching front, as noted in previous chapters, many schools have SDG-oriented degrees, such as Aston Business School's (UK) Master's degree in Social Responsibility and Sustainability or Monash Business School's (Australia) Master's degree in Indigenous Business Leadership. The BSc Accountancy and Financing course at Birmingham

Business School (University of Birmingham, UK) incorporates climate change throughout. The course directors explained that:

> Greta Thunberg was correct in what she said in Glasgow. It is an undisputable fact that business cannot carry on as normal if we are to effectively fight climate change and reach the government's target of net-zero carbon emissions by 2050. This means that every student studying accountancy and finance should know how to account for climate change.

They continue: 'Mainstreaming climate change into the syllabus just makes sense. Climate change is a real threat to business resilience, as well as the world at large, and nothing will change if we don't give our students the tools they need' (University of Birmingham, 2022).

Nottingham Trent University (UK) demonstrates the value of a cross-disciplinary programme with their Carbon Literacy Training for Educators, Communities, Organizations and Students being recognized in the sustainability category of the Wharton-QS Reimagine Education 2021 Awards. It is organized by the business school, together with the University Green Academy. All these examples acknowledge the tensions inherent to the SDGs. They are not considering the SDGs in an instrumental manner, that is, they are not considered as a commercial means to gain profit. They are seen as a mindset, and they go beyond what matters for the competitive advantage of firms. One can argue that, beyond their strict content, their aim is, as put by Kurucz et al. (2014: 449), to 'foster a common public discourse and prepare students to be critical thinkers and engaged citizens'. Chapter 3, on responsible management and leadership education and learning, provided a range of ideas and suggestions on how this can happen. Once again, though, rewards and incentives need to be aligned as this is more than just refreshing a few programmes. This is about letting go of courses/units that have been running for years and configuring new ones. Some current management theories frequently taught have to be relocated to history books. Amongst them are those that, for instance, privilege shareholders at the expense of others, or are steeped in anthropocentric thinking that considers humans as superior to anything else in the ecosystem, or that businesses are separate from the ecological world. They also include those that do not consider collaboration an option, where it is all about superior performance, manipulating stakeholders or competing to win. They also include traditional rational thinking logics, which purport that humans can make linear decisions and ignore the interconnected web of forces and the complex system we operate in.

Rejoining the earlier argument, it is about being clear in the performance standards used in business schools that some aspects of scholarship are more important than others. A way forward could be to borrow from the Canadian Corporate Knights Better World MBA annual ranking. This ranking is broad ranged. It includes elements such as the integration of sustainability into core courses, research and specialist institutes and centres, as well as faculty gender and racial diversity (Jack, 2022); to which we can add, as we just suggested, the number of SDGs-oriented articles published.

There are also some promising examples of great stewardship on the governance front. Some schools are also explicitly moving their form of governance, for instance, by committing to public value (for example, Cardiff Business School in the UK). Some schools are committing to tackling climate change in their operations by adopting carbon-neutral targets (for example, EDHEC Business School in France, or Rotterdam School of Management in the Netherlands). Darden School of Business, USA, already achieved net-zero emissions in 2018, thanks to partnering with a local renewal energy solar power company (Jack, 2022). The London School of Economics (LSE) is also providing much inspiration in its actions and its application to consultation so that there is broad adoption of the principles. Its Vice-Chancellor, Minouche Shafik, developed in 2020 a 'green strategy' and this involved consultation with students and staff. The strategy is about shaping the debate through research; embedding sustainability across teaching; promoting the green agenda externally; using sustainability to guide investment decisions; working in collaboration to further the green agenda, and ensuring that the LSE's own buildings are as environmentally friendly as possible (Ellis, 2021). It is claimed that the LSE became the first carbon-neutral university in the UK, but the Vice-Chancellor acknowledges that the LSE is transitioning, and part of its operations are still SDG-friendly.

Manchester (UK) have embedded the SDGS through, for instance, their procurement activities. They explain that they promote 'best purchasing practice and a responsible procurement approach by giving due weight to economic, social and environmental issues within purchasing activity' (Manchester University, 2022). They also have a strong statement regarding modern slavery and human trafficking; and have declared that they will end investments in fossil fuel reserve and extraction companies by 2022 and 'decarbonize' all investments by 2038 (Manchester

University, 2020). Reflecting on the comment by Patrick Deane (Queen's University Principal and Vice-Chancellor) that 'the first 16 SDGs point to the areas in which we want to have impact. The 17th tells us what the whole project is really all about: acting in community for the communal good', we noted that what seems to be missing a great deal from business schools' activities listed on their website is a description of their community outreach. If they are 'acting in community for the communal good', this outreach is driven essentially by students or a few passionate staff, rather than being embedded in the schools' operations. One can easily surmise that this will change if the THE Impact Rankings that assessed universities' achievement in delivering the SDGs gain visibility. Outreach is one of these measures. These rankings state that outreach 'is critical in higher education, and the work that universities do with their local, regional, national and international communities is another key way that they can have an impact on sustainability' (Times Higher Education, 2021).

One of the key aspects of governance and sustainability is whether schools have a holistic understanding of their activities. Are they organized so that they make things happen? Ad hoc changes and initiatives, while commendable and often motivating, may not lead to a transformational change. Teaching, research and operations must be aligned to meet the sustainability orientation.

CONCLUSION

To close, we think it might be helpful that business schools collaborate rather than compete on SDG issues and that all the stakeholders that make up the business school ecosystem actually work directly with the UN to gain guidance. All schools need to carry out an audit of their SDGs activities, and when they have done so they need to draw a clear, 'milestoned' plan with explicit deliverables so that they are accountable. Business schools' strategies need to be precise so that they can be scrutinized, and render it impossible for schools to superficially commit to the SDGs and view them as a tick-list exercise, rather than a transformational phenomenon. They need to 'walk the walk' and move beyond claiming teaching or research-related SDGs-siloed achievements. The adherence to the SDGs needs to permeate throughout the business schools and not be limited to a few specific examples of curricula or research studies. They have to practice what they preach. This may involve 'developing green campuses, creating healthy workplaces, divesting from fossil

fuel-laden portfolios and pension plans, and improving community relations' (Moratis and Melissen, 2022).

Finally, maybe, echoing Moratis and Melissen (2021: 7), we could
propose that to make things move, business schools could have a 'SDG
activist' in residence who 'challenges policies, administrators, educators,
and students, and thereby influences decision-making toward policy and
learning outcomes', in so doing they would facilitate the acceptance and
legitimization of the SDG agenda within business schools. This is an
existential issue as famously Nelson Mandela declared that 'education
is the most powerful weapon which you can use to change the world'.
And to end this chapter, we underline how: 'Education is the key to elim-
inating gender inequality, to reducing poverty, to creating a sustainable
planet, to preventing needless deaths and illness, and to fostering peace'
(USAID, 2013).

6. Equality/equity, diversity and inclusion

This chapter focuses on equality/equity, diversity and inclusion (EDI) in the context of building sustainable business schools, that is, schools that value difference, promote equality/equity and practise inclusion in respect of their academic staff, students and alumni. Equality and equity are distinct concepts in the theory and practice of managing diverse workforces, and different organisations will have a preference regarding which one drives strategy in this space. For the purposes of convenience, we use the acronym EDI to cover both, since some business schools favour the term equity, others equality. Addressing EDI is crucial to the success and sustainability of business schools in their roles as employers, producers of knowledge, educators of students, voices contributing to public debate and social change, and as role models of inclusive attitudes and behaviours. In recognition of this, accrediting bodies and ranking systems require and encourage the reporting of EDI metrics.

In their commitment statement on diversity, equity, inclusion (see Box 6.1 for definitions) and belonging, the AACSB (2021c) notes that it collects data on diversity trends with the goal of enabling its members to benchmark themselves against others. It is an explicit expectation of accredited schools that they will 'demonstrate a commitment to advancing diversity and inclusion issues in the context of the cultural landscape in which it operates' and 'foster awareness, understanding, acceptance, and respect for diverse viewpoints related to current and emerging issues' (AACSB, 2021c: 15). For the AACSB, the desired outcome of managing EDI in business schools is to foster a sense of belonging – 'a feeling of safety, acceptance, and being valued in social, group, work, and community settings' (AACSB, 2021c) – on-campus and online amongst staff and students. The FT Global MBA rankings are informed by data on gender diversity in schools (for example, percentage of women on MBA advisory boards, and percentage of female MBA students and staff members). The Canadian Corporate Knights Better World MBA ranking – as noted in Chapter 5 – includes faculty gender and racial diversity in its assessments (Jack, 2022). And the THE Impact rankings, configured around the SDGs, measure university research on gender equality (SDG 5), their own policies on gender quality, and their commitment to recruiting and promoting women.

BOX 6.1   AACSB DEFINITIONS OF DIVERSITY, EQUITY AND INCLUSION

AACSB defines diversity as culturally embedded identities rooted in historical and cultural traditions, legislative and regulatory concepts, ethnicity, gender, sexual orientation, socioeconomic conditions, religious practices, age, ability, and individual and shared experiences. When these differences are both recognized and respected through the delivery of high-quality business education, diversity becomes a powerful catalyst for unleashing the potential of an organization and individuals.

AACSB defines equity as providing access to high-quality business education globally. We recognize that, because we do not all share the same background, we have a responsibility to make sure that all individuals can grow, develop, and pursue their full potential through education.

AACSB defines inclusion as the opportunity for all individuals to participate. Inclusion requires that we empower people to respect and appreciate what makes us different.

Source: AACSB, 2021c: 3.

EDI is an area where business schools still have work to do, despite signs of progress. Commentaries and academic studies regularly point to the relative lack of women and racial and ethnic minorities in university and business school leadership positions (Bartel, 2018; Yousafzai, 2021), a gender pay gap in universities (see, for instance, UCEA, 2021), and cross-cultural challenges involved in internationalizing MBA curricula (Brocklehurst et al., 2007; Robinson, 2006; Sturdy and Gabriel, 2000, inter alia). Tienari and Taylor (2019: 949) note that 'publishing, teaching, institutional work and building reputation are all made more difficult for women, by men or by abstracts like culture, structure or masculinities', with the result that many women in universities and business schools experience disadvantage or marginalization, or feel undervalued or excluded.

Yet in many national jurisdictions, managing EDI is part of a set of legal requirements for employers to provide employees with work environments that are free of direct and indirect (sex, age and other forms of) discrimination and to ensure equality/equity and respectful workplace behaviours. Fostering greater diversity in the workforce body and promoting more inclusive practices have been shown in many (though not all) studies to improve individual employee, team and organizational outcomes (Calvard, 2020; Nkomo et al., 2019). To reach these outcomes requires more than a compliance-driven approach to EDI in which checklists of diversity markers are ticked off for reporting purposes. The diversity literature tells us that EDI is a vehicle for organizational learning, development and transformation, and should ideally be treated as such (Roberts and Mayo, 2019).

CONNECTING EDI AND SUSTAINABILITY

Our point of departure is that business schools that value and respect difference, promote gender, racial and other forms of equality and equity, and demonstrate inclusive practices in their offices, classrooms and public spaces are more sustainable. The diversity we have in mind is both *demographic* (in terms of an individual's social group/identity affiliations, such as gender, race or ethnicity, age, socioeconomic background and so on) and *epistemic* (about knowledges and ways of knowing promulgated in research and education). Questions about the demographic diversity (or not) of business schools may include these. What is the profile of academics, or MBA cohorts, by gender, race, or research/industry background? Who is in the leadership team? What are the barriers to career development facing academic staff from culturally and linguistically diverse backgrounds? Questions about the epistemic diversity (or not) of business schools may include these. What are the dominant forms of knowledge brought into the management classroom? Whose knowledge is excluded? How could students benefit from a greater diversity of perspectives on ways of managing and organizing? Whose voices need to be brought into the business school? What sustainability topics are researchers investigating, using what methodologies and with whom? We resist the temptation to assume that greater demographic diversity in business schools will necessarily generate greater epistemic diversity. After all, dominant ways of producing management knowledge (for example, positivist, large-scale survey work) are not the preserve of certain social groups or particular research topics, including sustainability.

The EDI–sustainability link can be made in at least three ways. First, EDI concerns are directly linked to some of the UN SDGs, as noted previously with respect to gender equality (SDG 5), but also good health and wellbeing (SDG 3), quality (inclusive and equitable) education (SDG 4), decent work and economic growth (SDG 8) and life on land (SDG 15). Second, more diverse knowledges and ways of knowing are needed to combat and address pressing societal issues, as advocated and demonstrated by scholarly work from the humanities and social sciences (Wright, 2019). Climate change (linked to climate action, SDG 13), for example, is a phenomenon that is experienced differently by different groups, with the rural poor and farmers, women, and children in so-called developing countries at greater risk of its effects than others (Tadaki et al., 2014; Watson and Huntington, 2014). Yet their experiences and adaptive practices are often overlooked in climate change treaties and policy, in market-based and/or technology-driven solutions, and in business school debates (Wright et al., 2022). We need to listen and learn from precisely these groups. Third, greater demographic and epistemic diversity in business schools ensures their futures by securing more relevant knowledge bases for research and teaching about societal grand challenges, thus strengthening their cognitive and moral legitimacy as social actors. As Samson et al. (2021: 435) point out, 'a diverse workforce will be more likely to be open-minded to a broader vision of sustainable development approaches'. Facets of EDI can be managed in such a way as to produce sustainable connections amongst diverse staff, and between staff and their employers, improving the social fabric of the business school and the work engagement and well-being of its staff and students.

EDI is not a universal construct; each of these terms has its own history, evolution and meaning. What constitutes a 'diverse group' depends on, inter alia, national context, history, patterns of migration, and the racial and religious make-up of a society. Given the EDI focus, it is vital that we provide a short reflexive note about *our own* identities and the places from which we write. We are three white academics working in conditions of privilege in business schools in Australia and France that are well integrated into the global system of business and management education. Our knowledges and experiences of EDI are therefore partial and reflective of our own Western values and biographies. We are wary of our use of terms like 'gender', or of assuming that 'women' or 'female academic', for instance, are universal categories of meaning or experience. The examples given and recommendations made in this chapter on EDI should thus not be treated as universal prescriptions for easy transposition into different locations. Rather, they are culturally located pieces of knowledge that may be taken up, adapted, translated, or otherwise, by readers in their particular contexts. We are aware of the selective nature of the examples we have given, and the challenges we have drawn attention to.

GENDER AND RACIAL EQUALITY AND DIVERSITY: KEY CHALLENGES

Professor Erika H. James is the first woman and the first person of colour to become the Dean of the Wharton School in its near 140-year history. This statement is a celebration of Professor James's outstanding achievements. But it is also a marker of the limits to gender and racial diversity that have historically, and in some cases still today, characterized business schools and universities in many global locations. Pictures of the all-white male line-up of the recipients of six honorary doctorates at the University of Melbourne in 2022 are a case in point. It provoked widespread consternation, and the withdrawal of research funding support from a major donor. Turning to the business school context, gender diversity is framed conventionally (and using contestable binary logic – more below) as a question of the gender balance between male and female academics, and in MBA cohorts. Here there is progress, but within limits. Wittenberg-Cox (2020), in a piece in Forbes with the headline 'Business schools are balancing at last', showed that over half of the top 20 (US) schools had balanced their MBA student populations. By balance is meant a maximum of 60 per cent of any gender in that population. Furthermore, a AACSB (2021d) examination of gender and racial demographic data on staff and students of US member schools from 2011–12 through to 2020–21 showed some progress. It showed:

- a 5 per cent increase (from 6 to 11 per cent) of black students enrolled in doctoral programmes;
- a 5 per cent increase (from 29 to 34 per cent) in female full-time faculty representation;
- a 5 per cent increase in female student representation in MBA programmes;
- a 7 per cent increase (from 19 to 26 per cent of total faculty population) in under-represented ethnicity groups among faculty.

In a CABS commentary piece (https://charteredabs.org/making-the-most -of-the-moment-gender-equality-in-business-and-management-schools/), Remke and her co-authors highlighted the strong vertical gender segregation of European business schools, manifest in the under-representation of women at all disciplines and academic levels, including the professoriate, in senior leadership roles including deans (McTiernan and Flynn, 2011) and in gatekeeping positions (for example, editorial roles) in academic fields (Metz et al., 2016). At the time of writing, the ongoing EU-funded TARGETED-MPI project (https://targeted-mpi.eu/) which includes these authors is examining how gender equality challenges identified in business schools can be tackled and changed. According to the research team, these challenges include a lack of transparency in business school hiring practices and promotions, and gender inequalities in research collaboration and in teaching allocations. The disproportionate impact of the pandemic on academic women's working lives, including a noted decrease in women's research outputs, is a further problem. The noted competitive, individualistic and hyper-masculine cultures of some business schools, where research is a game to be played, or teaching loads are negotiable, is the cultural fishbowl that arguably contributes to these negative gendered outcomes (Tienari and Taylor, 2019).

Gender inequality was also found in an examination of the business and management-related research impact case studies submitted to the UK REF in 2014 (Davies et al., 2019). The authors established that only 25 per cent of cases were led by women, a reflection of a gender bias in research impact work, and perhaps a lack of opportunity and support for women in this space. As noted in Chapter 4, the rising importance of creating research impact comes together with an expectation that business academics will undertake greater media and industry engagement, perhaps even the expectation that we need to be more social media savvy. Yet Savigny's (2019) work highlights a further challenge at the intersection of gender and race. In part through personal experience, Savigny found that when women, and in particular women of colour, speak in the public sphere as experts on their subjects, they often encounter what she calls 'cultural sexism', and forms of gendered and racialized violence (for example, online trolling, or worse) with pernicious effects on their well-being.

As for the student body, Fraser and Watson (2020) found that 'women only make up 40% of students in the field of business and management' and they highlight the need for 'gender diversifying' business curricula. Perhaps this lack of gender parity in the field is no surprise given that studies have found gender and diversity barriers in the visible commit-ments manifest in some business school promotional activity. Perriton, Elliott and Humbert (2022), for example, conducted a content analysis of the units advertised as comprising the content of 112 UK undergraduate and postgraduate management degrees, and found a significant gap in coverage of gender topics. In an earlier piece (apparently) based on the same dataset and published by CABS (n.d.b.), it was reported that Elliott and Perriton identified the high degree of absence of diversity in visual portrayals. Specifically, they found that:

> only 15% of programmes explicitly mentioned diversity in their publicly accessible module descriptions; an even smaller percentage of UG (8.5%) and PGT (6.7%) programmes included core diversity modules; and that only a single module in the 2,735 programmes audited made mention of disability issues (emphasis in the original).

The relative lack of attention to disability and neurodiversity, age and ageing, and social class, compared to gender, cultural diversity, and race and ethnicity, in the suite of EDI topics of relevance to business schools is noteworthy.

Returning to gender, Wittenberg-Cox's (2020) celebration of the bal-ancing of top 20 US schools' student body is tempered by her comment that less progress has been made in respect of gender balance amongst faculty. She calls for nothing less than culture change in business schools, since the relative imbalance of male to female staff has an impact on 'what gets taught, prioritised, researched', with the author noting 'little if any mainstreaming of gender education into core MBA curriculums' (Wittenberg-Cox, 2020). A more specific and epistemic aspect of this challenge is the relative lack of women's voices and women's writings in business and management curricula and theoretical canons – be it as research respondents, protagonists in teaching cases or textbooks, or as management and organizational theorists. Feminist scholars, and others, teach us that women's knowledges are often undervalued and/or written out or silenced from many dominant scholarly canons (including busi-ness and management) in the humanities and social sciences (Phillips et al., 2014), and that these are historically the preserve of white men and Eurocentric theorizing (Connell, 2007).

Kelan and Dunkley Jones's (2010) examination of MBA students' talk about gender suggests that a postfeminist climate is at work in management education with deleterious consequences for gender mainstreaming. Students talked in two predominant ways, according to the study – one that accepted the status quo of gender inequality, and another that gender does not matter. Given this insight, the potential for women from non-dominant societal groups (for example, Indigenous women, in the Australian context) to feature as writers of management theory, as employers or employees in case studies, or as a specific gender group is even less rosy and needs attention.

It is imperative to state (the obvious!) that reporting gender diversity in terms of a male–female binary is problematic. First, the binary is restrictive for those staff and students who do not conform to dominant (Western) gender norms, identifying as neither male or female, or who may be transitioning from one gender identity to another, or refute any. Business schools and universities more broadly can be contexts in which transgender, or gender-fluid employees may experience discrimination or alienation (O'Shea, 2017). Studies of LGBTIQA+ employees note the psychological costs that may come with decision-making about whether to disclose one's identity, or identities, in heteronormative or heterosexist workplaces, sometimes out of fear of a poor response from colleagues (Ozturk and Rumens, 2014). Secondly, the concept of intersectionality highlights the importance of viewing 'more than one difference at once' when seeking to understand how discrimination is experienced. Black and other feminist scholars (Acker, 2006; Crenshaw, 1989) remind us that the experiences of black women are not the same as those of white women, since structures of gender and race, and indeed also class, intersect differently to produce different life opportunities and outcomes. To be trite, not all women are the same, and especially so in a global context where transnational feminist struggles navigate a heterogeneity of aims, local contexts, strategies and tactics (Mohanty, 2003).

GENDER AND RACIAL EQUALITY AND DIVERSITY: BUSINESS SCHOOL RESPONSES IN PRINCIPLE AND PRACTICE

What is being done? What is to be done? Tienari and Taylor (2019: 949) state that 'evidence and analysis suggests some straightforward ways to "understand and dismantle" this sex-based inequality: first, acknowledge that it exists and is real; second, practice differently – all of us'. The burgeoning management and human resources literature on diversity and inclusion offers many insights into policies and practices that organisations – business schools included – may take to address gender and racial inequalities. Broadly speaking, it takes strong, committed and visible leadership on the importance to the school of diversity and inclusion, and actions to tackle issues and change current structures and policies, especially in respect of unfair or discriminatory practices. Bisoux (2021) offers a six-point action plan to 'elevate the equity curve' for business schools. These six points are: embrace inclusive leadership; get serious about mentoring; counteract unconscious bias; expand job candidate pools; fix broken talent pipelines; empower men to be allies. A 2016 EFMD report on the 'Gender gap in European business schools: A leadership perspective' (https://efmdglobal.org/wp-content/uploads/ EFMD_Gender_Gap_Report_2016.pdf) also called on business school leaders to take five steps to translate gender equality beliefs and commitment into gender diversity:

• Seek out, listen to, and learn from the experiences of female faculty members.
• Provide clear, unequivocal visible support and responsibility for all gender diversity initiatives.
• Take seriously the risk of gender bias in formulation and application of hiring, tenure, promotion criteria.
• Professionalise work on gender diversity in business schools.
• Enlist multiple stakeholders.

The ongoing EU-funded study led by Professor Claire Leitch, Dean of Lancaster University Management School (LUMS) Targeted-MPI Project – Transparent and resilient gender equality through integrated monitoring, planning and implementation – could be used to prompt discussion amongst business school leaders. Its aim is to improve gender equality in business schools by implementing and monitoring Gender Equality Plans (GEPs). Such plans would involve 'tasks and practices that address issues of discrimination such as slowed career progression, gender pay gap, lack of women in leadership positions' (https://targeted -mpi.eu/). GEPs have benchmarks for improvement and make use of outside monitoring.

Further specific actions could include: increasing the number of female and non-dominant group role models in business education; broadening or improving the scope/flexibility of leave provisions (for example, family leave, menstrual leave, intimate partner violence leave); training on unconscious bias (for example, as linked to recruitment and selection) or inclusive leadership; targeted recruitment; mentoring (including reverse mentoring, for example, where senior staff are mentored by junior staff on a particular topic); promoting allyship/allyship training and employee affinity groups (for example, in the LGBTIQA+ domain), and building networks. The Forté Foundation, for instance, has created a set of guidelines for male allies of women to support gender equity (http://www.fortefoundation.org/site/PageServer?pagename =allies#:~:text=In%202016%2C%20Fort%C3%A9%20launched%20a ,in%20working%20toward%20gender%20equity).

There are known challenges in utilizing these tools to manage EDI, however. For example, 'fix the women' approaches to gender equality, which place the onus on the individual employee to upgrade her (for example, negotiation) skills and networks, rather than tackling systemic barriers, do not fully tackle entrenched issues within the organization. Indeed, they may even be considered an abrogation of organizational responsibility for the issues at hand. And, according to Samson et al. (2021: 420), 'research also indicates that minorities, as well as women, are much less likely than white men to develop mentoring relationships'.

POSITIVE EXAMPLES

When it comes to positive examples from business schools, the websites of many leading schools variously contain clear statements, initiatives, action plans, role-holders and resources to promote diversity, equality/ equity and inclusion. Besides Erika James's leadership, the Wharton School has achieved a balance of women in the 2023 MBA class, and has a Wharton Male Allies project as part of its Gender Equality Initiative. The Cambridge Judge Business School formed an EDI committee in 2021 and set a long-term commitment to 'adapt our admissions, student orientation, and the curriculum so that they embrace the principles of equity, diversity, and inclusion' (https://www.jbs.cam.ac.uk/aboutus/ equality-diversity-and-inclusion/). The school has a dedicated manager and an action plan that sets out: to celebrate and embed EDI in all activities; to profile equality, diversity and under-representation; and to support expertise in business EDI research and teaching. INSEAD has an Equity, Diversity and Inclusion Taskforce, and an Executive Director Resources. The school has a Gender Initiative and also a Wealth Inequality Initiative. The Gender Initiative at Harvard Business School, led by Professor Robin J. Ely, has projects, educator resources and executive education. The University of Melbourne's Business School, together with its Faculty of Business and Economics, launched a strategy in 2021 to improve gender balance and equity through action plans in priority areas. The first is through the recruitment, development, support and promotion of more women to senior academic and leadership positions. The second is by placing a particular focus on negating the unconscious bias that may affect recruitment, the structure of workloads, responsibilities for leadership positions and, more broadly, 'to reflect critically on what it takes to be a successful academic' (https://mbs.edu/news/how-were -improving-gender-equity-among-business-academics).

Dedicated research centres and topics can also make a difference. The Suliman S. Olayan School of Business at the American University of Beirut, Lebanon, for instance, has a noteworthy Centre for Inclusive Business and Leadership (CIBL), and a Women in Data Science (WiDS) initiative and webinar. WiDS sets out to give 'a platform for data scientists in the Arab Middle East to promote a higher representation of women in data science'. As for CIBL, its focus is on creating inclusive and systemic change for women in organizational and societal contexts. One way of pursuing this goal is to produce gender- and sector-disaggregated data in the specific context of the Arab MENA (Middle East and North Africa) region where such important data are lacking. These data are vital to address gender inequality 'through mechanisms that balance between increasing labor force participation and ensuring dignified work. On every relevant index, women's economic participation and workplace protection [in the MENA context] is the worst across the world' (https:// www.aub.edu.lb/cibl/Pages/aboutcibl.aspx). SDGs-related research can also mainstream gender, as illustrated, for example, by recent works on gender and corporate social responsibility, or gender, human rights and supply chains (Grosser et al., 2017; Grosser, 2021).

Oxford University's Saïd Business School reportedly pursues a diversity and inclusion plan that involves its policies, culture, and classrooms. A Women at Oxford Saïd initiative for students and the Oxford Women's Leadership Development Programme are also features. A particular scholarship programme – the Laidlaw Scholarships – enables the business school to 'build on its position as Europe's most gender balanced major business school'. Furthermore, it has a strategy on racism that comes from the work done by its Anti-Racism Taskforce. Its three-step approach was adopted by the 2019–20 MBA class to Listen, Learn, Lead, with an associated video. Saïd's website also demonstrates its support of Black History Month, a commitment to disability inclusion, and its Pride@SBS initiative. International Day Against Homophobia, Biphobia, Intersexphobia and Transphobia (IDAHOBIT) is celebrated in over 130 countries, including at Monash Business School (Australia), where staff and students take part in a week of on-campus events and celebrations, story-sharing, and raising the Pride Flag on each of its campuses during Monash Pride Week.

Beyond the strategies and action plans of individual business schools, accrediting bodies and other institutions, actors provide commentaries with suggestions, resources and materials for more gender-balanced and racially aware classrooms and curricula. The PRME Working Group on Gender Equality (Flynn et al., 2020) published an edited book called *Integrating Gender Equality into Business and Management Education*. It provides support and materials to integrate gender issues, awareness and knowledge into curricula and research. There is a Global Gender Equality Repository for management education. PRME's 'Best 10 Lists' features academic articles on particular topics (including business and human rights, responsible management, climate change and responsible finance) that are considered best. Dutch academic Yvonne Benschop's (2021) article 'Grand challenges, feminist answers' is on the list and worthy of reading. Fraser and Watson (2020) offer advice on how to 'gender diversify' the business curriculum. They underscore the importance of teaching more 'gender-diverse' cases, recommending Harvard Business Publishing which has a webpage with specific cases that feature female protagonists. They also pointed to Lesley Symons' development of The Case for Women, which addresses the lack of women in case studies used in business education (https://www.worldcommercereview .com/html/symons-the-case-for-women.html). Kristin Williams's (2022) book *Historical Female Management Theorists: Frances Perkins, Hallie Flanagan, Madeleine Parent, Viola Desmond* offers an alternative set of readings to the male-dominated canon of Taylor, Fayol, Mayo and so on.

Anti-Racist and Decolonizing Business and Management

In an earlier section, we highlighted examples of business schools' concerns to enhance the racial diversity of staff and students. Some are also committing to racial equality and anti-racism through statements aligned to the Black Lives Matter Movement, by reviewing reading lists or curricula to see how representative they are of texts, ideas or theories from non-white (/male) writers, or, particularly in the British context, by contributing to broader university agendas to decolonize their institutions and recognize their colonial histories (for example, the University of Glasgow). Building the Anti-Racist Classroom (BARC; https://

barcworkshop.org/) is an international collective of women business and management educators of colour who have created an approach to anti-racist pedagogy and practice for use in higher educational, and especially business school contexts. The collective has developed workshops which they have delivered into several institutions. They have collated together materials and blogs to enable others to take up the struggle for racial justice in their classrooms. One member of the collective, Dr Angela Martinez Dy, from Loughborough University London Business School, has played a key role in the development of an innovative anti-racism strategy in her own institution. Readers might consider watching this YouTube video (https://www.youtube.com/watch?v=lWQbWizLFAA) in which Dr Martinez Dy explains her vision for an anti-racist university and race equality guiding principles. Loughborough University's Race Equality Charter (REC) commitments include: improved diversity in leadership positions; a cultural shift; attract and maintain black staff; tackle defensiveness in response to data; increase confidence in raising and responding to racist incidents; transform the student experience for black and minority ethnic students; provide a better experience for black graduate research students. The University's work on race equity won it an award from the UK's Advance HE.

As the renaming of Cass Business School to Bayes Business School – covered in Chapter 3 – indicates, the history of business and management in both theory and practice is intimately connected to the history of colonialism and capitalism (Westwood and Jack, 2009). Much of what we take, and teach, as management practice, including a host of accounting, taxation and other commercial practices, has an oft-unacknowledged colonial history linked, for example, to the management of slavery plantations (Cooke, 2003) or the racialized and racist public and legal administration of Indigenous peoples and their lands (Moreton-Robinson, 2015), whose legacies and practices continue today. The current system of management education is an unequal one. The Global North remains a key market for international student flows, while the global expansion of management education has been characterized by the institutionalization of Angle-American MBA programmes (Houldsworth et al., 2019), and the diffusion, imitation and adaptation of US management knowledge and pedagogy through business schools elsewhere. This system is viewed by some as propagating new and ongoing forms of colonization through practices such as the creation of international branch campuses and the use of culturally specific and often ethnocentric US/European textbooks, curricula and theoretical frameworks in non-Western locations (Joy and Poonamallee, 2013; Kothiyal et al., 2013; Liang and Wang, 2004).

The consequences of this flow from the centre to the peripheries of global management education can be challenging. Kothiyal et al. (2013), for example, found that academic staff at Indian business schools experience feelings of ambivalence, and pressures to mimic Western theoretical, methodological and pedagogical practices in ways that 'mute' their own scholarly activities. A similar ambivalence at the level of business school strategy in India was identified by Vakkayil and Chatterjee (2017), who found that schools had to navigate the cultural, epistemic and material challenges of choosing between conformity and distinctiveness in the context of accreditation and other pressures for globalization. And in the South African context, Nkomo (2015) noted that the post-colonial, post-apartheid context and the socioeconomic development needs of the state shape significantly the aspirations of business schools and the dilemmas they face in adopting non-local frameworks and practices.

In the humanities and social sciences, there is a 'decolonial turn' (Mbembe, 2016) that broadly seeks to deconstruct these colonial dynamics. This turn has, slowly but surely, moved into the business school arena, in particular through calls to 'Decolonize the business school', with associated conferences, symposia, journal special issues, development of scholarly resources and teaching materials, and other forms of scholarly activism (Jammulamadaka et al., 2021). The creation of the Decolonizing Alliance is an important group of diverse scholars (as an alternative to the white, male, Anglo/European mainstream of management, including critical management) who 'support each other through collaboration, translation, active solidarity, and the sharing of material and educational resources wherever possible, and to be led by scholars from the Global South and scholars of colour from the Global North' (https://decolonizingalliance.wordpress.com/). The websites states that they are 'actively engaged in the development of interventions at international conferences, writing collaboratively, curating webinars and workshops, and a Palestinian Solidarity Working Group formed in 2021'. These resources are vital for business schools that might wish to consider a more radical agenda for their sustainability work.

CONCLUSION

This chapter has underscored the importance of equality/equity, diversity and inclusion as a set of sustainability challenges and issues that business schools must address in their research, education and operations. The focus of the chapter has predominantly been on gender and racial equality and diversity and has covered the continuing issues of gender and racial inequality in business schools, and the strategies and actions in place to remedy them. There is much work to be done, especially recognizing that the global management education system is hierarchically structured and that business schools themselves are sources of cultural and racial hierarchy. The work ahead is hard, but it must be tackled for business schools to become beacons of sustainability, and homes to sustain and engage workforces, student cohorts and alumni.

7.   Reflection and conclusion

We started writing this book when Melbourne was in the midst of what became the world's longest lockdown due to the COVID-19 pandemic, and Europe and the US were getting used to living with the virus and taking for granted that it would not be eliminated. The lockdowns are in the past, but COVID-19 is not. People are still getting sick and dying, and each time a new variant is announced we start wondering, what next? What if? While we cannot answer these questions, we are certain of one thing: the SDGs are as relevant as ever if not more. The pandemic might have taken attention away from these issues for a little while, but they are still there. COP26, which took place during the height of the COVID-19 crisis, reminded us of that. It was a sharp reminder of the danger of ignoring the sustainability agenda, and the need for action at the institutional level. Before reflecting on the direct sustainability implications that the pandemic brought to the fore, it is worth contemplating one of the major changes that it brought upon us: the acceleration of online teaching and the use of technology in all aspects of education.

DIGITAL TRANSFORMATION AND THE SUSTAINABLE BUSINESS SCHOOL

While we have seen a significant and accelerating growth in the use of online technologies in higher education internationally over the last decade (Albert et al., 2021) the resultant social distancing surrounding COVID-19 meant a large-scale transition to online learning (Govindarajan and Srivastava, 2020) which continued between 2020 and 2021, and is still in place in many schools. In business schools, as in all other types of organization, 2020 called for leaders to be agile, pragmatic, and bold (Hofgartner, 2021). This represented a paradigm shift in the higher education environment where entire student bodies were abruptly shifted from face-to-face to remote instruction through the use of digital technologies, and faculty members had to adapt their courses in the face of lockdown at very short notice and with limited formal training (Krishnamurthy, 2020). For some academics this meant an overnight transition to using new technologies in their content delivery. It also meant a drastic change in the lives of students. For example, it resulted in a suspension of internships and study abroad periods. It often involved having to work from their student accommodation rooms or returning to their families. In some cases, international students were confined to hotel rooms waiting to travel home from their places of study, or waiting to come to the overseas business school they were planning to attend.

What this has meant for the management education sector, and for business schools in particular, is the need to acknowledge that the digital universe business schools operate in currently is here to stay for the long term, in some shape or another. It is now well recognized that online learning or e-learning plays and will continue to play a decisive role in supporting and engaging teaching and learning activities (Thangaiah et al., 2021). Online programs are the fastest-growing segment in management education (Morrissey, 2019). The move to emergency remote teaching due to COVID-19 provides a discontinuous disruption to business-as-usual for the sustainable business school. However, it must be recognized that what universities and business schools have been facing during COVID-19, and still are currently, is a stop-gap measure rather than a representative approach to what is required as digitalization within the sector evolves into a valuable instructional experience (Krishnamurthy, 2020). The future for business schools will require a shift from digital replacement to digital transformation.

Research undertaken in 2021 by AMBA and Business Graduates Association (BGA) in association with BARCO (digital solutions provider) explores business school leaders' views about technology, and on the applications of technology within business schools, examining how schools are adapting to a new era of education technology. The report evidences that in terms of the perceptions of the success of digital technology on business education:

- Fifty-two per cent of business school leaders believe that online teaching methods are 'the same as', 'somewhat better', or 'much better' than traditional classroom teaching.
- Forty-eight per cent admitted online teaching methods were 'somewhat worse' than a traditional classroom experience.

Whilst these figures suggest a split vote, the report also finds that 82 per cent of business school leaders are planning to invest more in technology over the next couple of years to further enable online teaching and learning. There are a variety of different approaches to pedagogy using online delivery, representing a matter of degree. Online delivery is a general term which covers: fully online: 80 per cent or more of course activities and interactions are online; hybrid or blended: between 30 and 79 per cent of course activities and interactions are online; web-facilitated: between 1 and 29 per cent of course activities and interactions are online; compared to traditional: 0 per cent (so no online components) (Albert et al., 2021; Allen et al., 2016).

As business schools evolve through the process of transformation, they have time to rethink and plan how they may approach digital transformation for the longer term. For the sustainable business school, key to evolving is seeing the future as an opportunity to reassess their overall approach to online learning and how technology may be employed to re-invent teaching, learning, assessment and certification (Krishnamurthy, 2020). Some commentators suggest that the problem at the heart of good digital learning is not technological but more one of organization (Frattini, 2021). This requires reflection on developing coherent student experiences that are built on sound instructional design principles where it should be ensured that pedagogy drives technology and not the other way round (Hofgartner, 2021). Those institutions that were best prepared for the digital transformation have already demonstrated that they understand that online teaching requires pedagogical models and approaches that are substantially different from traditional methods (Frattini, 2021). Digital technologies provide a platform for enhancing the value of students' education, particularly around value-in-development, but also in delivery and consumption through a shift from passive to interactive modes of delivery (Uncles, 2018). Designing an effective and quality online programme requires experience and knowledge in areas such as instructional design and the moderation of online sessions, in addition to the will and ability to train teaching staff to use these tools (Frattini, 2021). Consequently, reflection on the training efforts that are required for both faculty and students to facilitate a change in their mindsets as well as practices is required (Govindarajan and Srivastava, 2020). It is the role of those that govern business schools to drive innovation in the process of transformation, making innovation part of business school culture and values so that everyone is encouraged on board in the digital transformation journey (Hofgartner, 2021).

According to Uncles (2018), digital technologies and technology-enabled teaching and learning provide numerous opportunities for students and educators to engage actively both within and beyond the classroom. Collaborative hackathons, for example, are gaining traction to this end in many institutions. Employers are calling for work-ready and socially skilled graduates who can use current technology ethically and efficiently (Crittenden and Peterson, 2019). Perhaps more importantly for business school sustainability will be an acknowledgement of the need to embrace personalization of the learning process (Krishnamurthy 2020; Uncles, 2018). Already, students want to learn 'wherever' (for example, on board a plane), 'however' (for example, by playing a business game), and 'whenever' (for example, at 2 a.m.). They want to be able to choose what fits best their own needs (Schlegelmilch, 2020). Consequently, digital technology is now being applied to deliver world-class knowhow at a time and place convenient to the student (Morrissey, 2021). Such learning personalization will support diversity. Additionally, the pandemic emphasized the value of digital tools for inclusiveness such that new emphasis will be for students of the future to have access to multiple pathways to learn the same content (Krishnamurthy, 2020). For example, whether for health or work reasons, some students inevitably have to 'pause' their participation in a traditional, face-to-face training course. Digital training can have a great value in ensuring the continuity of the training path for those in difficult situations (Frattini, 2021). In line with the requirement for greater personalization and inclusivity, online delivery of education is also expanding rapidly to meet the career-specific education and training needs of adult populations (Tremblay et al., 2012). Emerging trends are micro-credentials, or digital badges which act as certification for online modules or courses. For example, Australia's RMIT University offers a range of micro-certificates and collaborates with KPMG, EY, and other companies, in delivery (Schlegelmilch, 2020).

Sustainable business schools will be those who recognize digital transformation as a lever to competitive advantage in front of the changing face of competition. Personalization is also fundamental for leveraging competitive advantage and aligns with the imperative for business schools to maintain and grow enrolment numbers either through an expansion in existing programmes or into geographically diverse markets with a wider mix of programme offerings and more varied channels of distribution (Uncles, 2018). Apart from competition from traditional areas, business schools need to design their future strategies taking into consideration the entry of specialized online education providers. Perhaps the most well known of such competitors is Coursera, which provides unlimited access to more than 7,000 courses, hands-on projects, and certificate programmes, for an all-inclusive subscription price. It charges business schools for placing their courses on their platform and incentivizes the school with up to 15 per cent of gross revenues received from subscribed learners (Schlegelmilch, 2020). While this form of competition is not new and was not the direct result of the COVID-19 pandemic, we are witnessing a host of new entries into this market.

In France, for example, L'ISCOD-CO Business School is a pioneer in 100 per cent online training. For 20 years, the school has been offering a range of exclusively work-based-study courses via digital learning. Each year, it trains 500 apprentices throughout France in the professions of commerce, marketing and communication, digital, human resources and management. The school relies on its internal recruitment agency to support companies looking for work-based-study students. This close collaboration with the world of work is also reflected in the content of the training provided, developed according to the needs identified by companies. In some cases, universities have founded their own special-ized provision, which they run as non-profit businesses, for example, edX founded by MIT and Harvard (Schlegelmilch, 2020). Additionally, we are witnessing the rise of social media organizations moving into the online learning space. LinkedIn Learning offers personalized course recommendations based on the skills and interests of member profiles through which courses are filtered and selected to suit member needs. Designing programmes which are constantly tuned to how students are transforming will be the imperative, and this includes particularly those who are not yet of an age to apply to university.

Collaboration has been an underlying theme throughout this book. The sustainable business school will embrace digitalization as a means of leveraging collaboration. This will have implications for the use and roles of faculty, placing greater emphasis on mentors and peer-to-peer learning (Krishnamurthy, 2020). Technology has the power to drive col-laboration and support successful learning outcomes ultimately bringing like-minded people together (Hofgartner, 2021). As world economies become increasingly interconnected, international skills have become ever more important for operating successfully on a global scale. This has led to growing demands to incorporate an international dimension into education and training. Digital transformation enables this.

However, digital transformation of business schools in terms of both content and delivery is not without its challenges. It necessitates schools keeping pace with rapid advances in communications and social net-working technologies; accommodating the increased costs of technology into existing mechanisms for financing higher education; and taking full advantage of the educational opportunities these technologies provide to expand student access and improve their success in higher education (Tremblay et al., 2012). Much of the digital learning methodologies, contexts and tools that business schools are using today are not new, even if we are witnessing a rise in their use. This is to a great extent due to the COVID-19 pandemic. However, to be sustainable, in future, business schools will have to become familiar with the potential of a myriad of developments that will further revolutionize the way students will learn and business schools will teach (Schlegelmilch, 2020). These will include a greater use of virtual reality as a method of teaching and learning, such as that pioneered at NEOMA Business School (France). We may also expect greater use of augmented reality and holographic technology to help in curriculum development to evidence how organizations may develop a more positive environmental impact (Schlegelmilch, 2020).

In addition, there is the potential for artificial intelligence (AI) to further promote personalization of learning such that both content and approach may be specifically tailored to the background and needs of an individual learner. Major online learning resources like Udacity, edX, and Coursera were born out of US AI laboratories and founded and/or headed by AI experts: Sebastian Thrun at Stanford (Udacity), Andrew Ng at Stanford (Coursera), and Anant Agarwal at MIT (edX) (https://www.onlineeducation.com/features/ai-in-distance-learning). There are currently three main types of AI in online learning: adaptive learning (education software that is customized to each student individually, such that concepts are presented in the order a particular student finds easiest to understand and are able to be completed at a self-set pace); intelligent tutoring systems (AI-powered solutions tailored to match each individual student's needs and abilities) and visual facilitators (AI-powered 3D environments and realistic virtual characters) (https://www.onlineeducation.com/features/ai-in-distance-learning).

While it is not the intention of this chapter to provide a full overview of all new and emerging digital technologies of value in education, these examples give a flavour of the opportunities to be grasped. Imagine combining all the different technologies in the design of innovative learning environments, which join online and offline environments in real space and virtual formats. We already have virtual teaching assistants in the form of IBM's Jill Watson. Jill Watson can answer questions about a course syllabus, when deployed on specialized online communication forums. It may be some time before such technologies appear as mainstream in business education, but business schools should be starting to direct their efforts and investments towards reconfiguring their physical spaces, and integrating digital tools so as to make it possible for simultaneous face-to-face lessons and distance learning to happen seamlessly (Frattini, 2021). However, it is worth reiterating that future innovations in AI-education must focus first and foremost on meeting the needs of the people who use it: teachers and students. Pedagogy drives technology, not vice versa, and a sustainably oriented business school cannot afford to lose this message. Technology is there to serve its stakeholders and help to achieve its SDG goals. Technology will enhance diversity and inclusions and has positive implications for environmental sustainability, not least the reduction of the carbon footprint.

While technology-based education has been highlighted as the immediate consequence of the pandemic, there are many more, not all of which can be deemed positive in terms of the SDGs.

PANDEMIC IMPLICATIONS AND SUSTAINABILITY-ORIENTED BUSINESS SCHOOLS

The pandemic has revealed the danger of the casualization of staff. As the National Tertiary Education Union of Australia explains:

> The predominance of insecure forms of employment in higher education not only has serious implications for the individual staff involved, where over 50% are looking to pursue an academic or research career, but it also raises questions about the sustainability of teaching arrangements offered and the quality of the student experience, in spite of the best intentions and ability of those precariously employed staff. (NTEU, 2022)

Half of the undergraduate teaching is done by casual staff, and '[b]y the May quarter of 2020, nearly 8000 casual jobs had already been shed from tertiary education. The loss of casual jobs accelerated, reaching 10,000 positions (relative to year-earlier levels) by late 2020' (Littleton, 2022: 12). This clearly highlights that casualization is, by and large, negative to people – and notably to women, as they form the majority of the workforce that lost their employment (Littleton, 2022) and to students, as the reliance on casual teaching staff can result in inferior teaching quality and is most unlikely to be the research-led education that top-tier business schools claim to offer to their students (Hommel and Hommel, 2020). How can business schools claim to teach sustainability when their operations are contradictory to it? It is in this regard that our implications on EDI really come to the fore. We fully embrace Jones's (2020) view that 'Competition and casualization now have to give way to fairness and social responsibility'.

The pandemic has also seen the gender gap increase in universities. For instance, when working from home, while the rate of writing papers by men grew by over 6 per cent, it grew by less than 3 per cent for women; and 'the proportion of women as authors on publications fell from 36 to 32% in that time. Women academics were registering their involvement on an even smaller proportion of research projects than men during the pandemic period than they were before it' (Betts, 2022). On both a sad and a positive note, some institutional players are also starting to make their mark and do not let pass obvious disregard of violation of the SDGs. They call out bad behaviour and inaction. For instance – while this is not in business schools, but in the medical faculty – The Snow Medical Research Foundation decided to withdraw its funding from the University of Melbourne, because of the 'unacceptable' decision of the University to award six of its highest honours to male professors, as noted in Chapter 6. 'In the last three years, not a single honorary doctorate has been awarded to women or someone of non-white descent' and, 'while it appears the policies on gender equality and diversity are in place, the outcomes do not align with the University's stated goals' (Snow Medical Research Foundation, reported by Campbell, 2022).

As seen in earlier chapters, while progress is slow, there are multiple examples of positive change. In education, we highlighted the increase of holistic Master's degrees (for instance, Aston Business School, UK) or postgraduate certificates in sustainability (for instance, University College Cork, Ireland) or even full MBAs (notably the Duquesne (USA) MBA on sustainable practices that seek to integrate sustainability in all aspects of business education and embrace the PRME principles). In terms of research, we saw that more and more institutional governmental funding agencies were looking for evidence of public impact (broadly defined). At the operational level, we are experiencing the increase of 'green' actions by business schools (for example, in their procurement) or efforts to increase gender and diversity throughout the business schools. We also explained that many business schools are signatories of the PRME principles, but up to now little had been done specifically about climate change. This is no more the case.

At COP26, an alliance 'Business Schools for Climate Leadership' was formed. The partners are Oxford Saïd Business School, Cambridge Judge

Business School, HEC Paris, IE Business School, IESE Business School, INSEAD, IMD and London Business School. They state that: 'As leading European business schools, the founding members recognize the responsibility in driving the acceleration of business activities towards the goals of the Paris Agreement and the UN Framework Convention on Climate Change' (Business Schools for Climate Leadership, 2022). Their declared goal is 'to equip present and future leaders to address climate change', and they explain that the alliance 'represents the beginnings of collective action across business schools starting with the founding members. As educators and researchers—as well as leading voices and stewards of powerful alumni bodies—we need to work together to incite, support, and mobilize our many stakeholders to protect humanity' (Business Schools for Climate Leadership, 2022). While this group is small, its members are elite schools, so we can expect that they will become role models, and others will want to be associated with them and as such follow their positive actions.

Climate change also became more salient an issue within business schools during the pandemic. Even ardent climate change sceptics are starting to acknowledge that the series of unprecedented climate events such as the 2022 Australian Queensland or New South Wales floods or the US 'bombogenesis' snowstorms may have to do with climate change. Why? Not only because of the various climate-related disasters (such as fires, heatwaves, floods, the melting of glaciers or the increase of the list of endangered animals due to the loss of habitat) that most countries are experiencing or that are now commonly reported on but also because of the dramatic reduction in travel and notably air travel. Travelling is, or, more correctly, used to be, part of business schools' academic life. The conference 'circuit' governed many academics' rhythm of working life (if not personal) and had career implications for many. It was rather usual for most academics to attend at least two conferences per year (often a general conference like a marketing conference and a specialized conference like a consumer marketing conference). Let us take an example. Many management researchers work through the end of the year on papers they can submit to the Academy of Management conference, arguably the largest and most prestigious management conference. Up to now, this conference took place in the USA. The acceptance rate is low, so many schools perceive that if your paper is accepted that you are clearly research active and aim to publish eventually in top-tier journals. August is when it happens, so many make sure they do not teach, so that they can attend and present their paper, and hence disseminate their research, but conferences are not just about that. This is a great learning environment, allowing you to attend development workshops that many schools do not offer. This may enhance, for instance, your writing or reviewing skills, or introduce you to new teaching methods. It is also the perfect networking environment, where for an early career researcher onwards you meet future colleagues and potential future employers. You may also meet potential new co-authors, allowing you to engage in new research projects. You may also get invited to give guest lectures or join editorial boards. This may lead to associate or full editorships and so on. You may also be asked to put your name down for elections for learned societies or conference positions. In short, such a conference is a conduit to show excellence in research, and to enhance career opportunities. COVID-19 and the closure of borders ensued. There was no way of going to the USA, either because the USA had closed their borders or because the academics' own country of work forbade overseas travel. Conferences turned into virtual events. Before thinking of the scholarly implications, business schools realized that they could save a huge amount of money (no airfares/accommodation/sustenance/insurance) and also that their carbon footprint was improving hugely. This sudden imposition of no travel brought to the fore how academics and their regular routine contributed to climate change. It also made many recruiters turn to virtual interviews, even post-restrictions, to keep cost and carbon waste down. This, of course, raises the question of whether one should keep the virtual format and not return to face-to-face because of the contribution of air travel to climate change. Planes consume a lot of energy and depend on fossil fuels. Their carbon emissions contribute greatly to the warming of the atmosphere. So, until there are massive technological advancements and flights become carbon emission neutral, shall we stop physical business and management academic conferences? Skiles et al. (2022) also argued that virtual conferences had other sustainability-oriented benefits. They showed they improved diversity, equity and inclusion.

For many, physical conferences were simply too expensive, which means that few conference attendees could come from poorer countries or institutions. They also did not give any flexibility. Women's participation was somewhat compromised because, being by and large the main carers in their community, some women did not have the opportunities to be away. Scholars with a disability were also limited in their opportunity to attend due to the lack of facilities. In short, we can argue that virtual conferences are more sustainability-friendly, but are they good for scholarship? Are they useful for career advancement and do we take the risk that, without them, gendered networks will be entrenched? This is one clear issue that business schools will have to face. Are hybrid events a solution? This is tough to know as they may only help the learning and dissemination of knowledge rather than the subtler issues of networking and learning the soft skills and developing the know-how and tacit knowledge needed to thrive in a business school environment.

This is a salient problem for all, but especially for doctoral and early-career researchers who need to find their way and navigate their career path. It is likely that in the short term a compromise will have to be adopted, that is, the reduction of conference travel, rather than its eradication. However, one can see, on balance, limited benefits from academics travelling the world and thereby burning carbon simply to attend a job interview or to give a one-hour speech. This is certainly one easy impactful change that business schools can make.

CONCLUSION

As we mentioned earlier, we wrote this book during the pandemic and by the time it is published we hope that the worst of the pandemic will way be well behind us. We also hope that any notion of a 'new normal' will be one where sustainability is an accepted and common point of reference for business schools, and not something to be debated or criticized as being 'idealistic'. We also think, as Jones (2020) did, that '[s]taff have already demonstrated their adaptability, intuitively and collegially doing what is right for their students. Now Covid-19 offers a chance for the sector to redefine its relationship with the public, and for university managers to reset their relationship with staff'. In short, the time is right for transformation; the pandemic may have been the silver lining for sustainability we needed. Using Thomas and Ambrosini's wording (2021: 264), we hope that our suggestions made throughout this book 'offer a way forward, and we hope that our "think piece" stimulates reflection and will generate conversation between management academics. Specifically, we hope that practices embracing our approach will be shared and new ideas will emerge.'

It is the duty of business schools not to leave behind their stakeholders, be it students or their stakeholders in industry and the community at large. The SDGs are a priority throughout the world, and business schools have the responsibility to educate students about them, to carry out research that will expand what they mean and how they can become a reality for all, be it individuals or organizations. The drivers are present, and are getting stronger, and there is no shortage of advice, including from books such as this one or from institutions such as the EFMD or the UN.

References

AACSB. 2020a. 2020 Guiding Principles and Standards for Business Accreditation. https://www.aacsb.edu/-/media/documents/accreditation/2020 -aacsb-business-accreditation-standards-marked-up-july-2021.pdf?rev=d7e 9a58a375d4928a62896017addbce3

AACSB. 2020b. Gender diversifying the curriculum. https://www.aacsb.edu/ insights/articles/2020/09/gender-diversifying-the-business-curriculum

AACSB. 2021a. Encouraging business schools to address societal impact. https:// www.aacsb.edu/insights/articles/2021/02/encouraging-business-scholars-to -address-societal-impact

AACSB. 2021b. Research that matters. An action plan for creating business school research that positively impacts society. AACSB Thought Paper 33. https://www.aacsb.edu/insights/reports/research-that-matters

AACSB. 2021c. Our commitment to diversity, equity, inclusion, and belonging. https://www.aacsb.edu/-/media/publications/research-reports/deib_positioning_ paper.pdf?rev=1876431c9287467f9395358b2810dfbf

AACSB. 2021d. Ethnicity and gender representation at US business schools. https://www.aacsb.edu/insights/publications/data-reports/ethnicity-and-gender -representation-at-us-business-schools

Acker, J. 2006. Inequality regimes: Gender, class, and race in organizations. *Gender and Society*, 20(4): 441–464.

Aguinis, H., Ramani, R. S., Alabduljader, N., Bailey, J. and Lee, J. 2019. A pluralist conceptualization of scholarly impact in management education: Students as stakeholders. *Academy of Management Learning and Education*, 18, 11–42.

Aguinis, H., Cummings, C., Ramani, R.S. and Cummings, T.G. 2020. 'An A is an A': The new bottom line for valuing academic research. *Academy of Management Perspectives*, 34(1): 135–154.

Akrivou, K. and Bradbury-Huang, H. 2015. Educating integrated catalysts: Transforming business schools toward ethics and sustainability. *Academy of Management Learning and Education*, 14(2): 222–240.

Alajoutsijärvi, K., Juusola, K. and Siltaoja, M. 2015. The legitimacy paradox of business schools: losing by gaining? *Academy of Management Learning and Education*, 14(2): 277–291.

Albert, S., Fulton, D. Ramanau, R. and Janes, A. 2021. Exploring cross-disciplinary differences in course mode, instructional tools and teaching methods in online courses in business and management. *The International Journal of Management Education*, 19(3): 100532.

Allen, E., Seaman, J., Poulin, R. and Straut, T. 2016. Online report card: Tracking online education in the USA. USA: Babson Survey Research

Group and Quahog Research Group. Retrieved 3 February 2021, from https:// onlinelearningsurvey.com/reports/onlinereportcard.pdf

Almeida, M.F.L.D. and Melo, M.A.C.D. 2017. Sociotechnical regimes, technological innovation and corporate sustainability: From principles to action. *Technology Analysis and Strategic Management*, 29(4): 395–413.

Altmetric. 2017. *Tips and Tricks: Promoting Your Research Online*. https://doi .org/10.6084/m9.figshare.5271979

AMBA (Association of MBAs). 2019. MBA accreditation criteria. https://www .associationofmbas.com/app/uploads/2019/09/MBA-criteria-for-accreditation .pdf

AMBA and Business Graduates Association (BGA) Education Technology Research, in association with Barco. 2021. https://www.associationofmbas .com/research/exclusive-amba-bga-research-examines-how-business-schools-are-adapting-to-a-new-era-of-education-technology/

Anderson, L., Ellwood, P. and Coleman, C. 2017. The impactful academic: Relational management education as an intervention for impact. *British Journal of Management*, 28(1): 14–28.

Antonacopoulou, E.P. 2010. Making the business school more 'critical': Reflexive critique based on phronesis as a foundation for impact. *British Journal of Management*, 21: S6–S25.

Antonacopoulou, E.P., Dehlin, E. and Zundel, M. 2011. The challenge of delivering impact: Making waves through the ODC debate. *Journal of Applied Behavioral Science*, 47(1): 33–52.

Awaysheh, A. and Bonfiglio, D. 2017. Leveraging experiential learning to incorporate social entrepreneurship in MBA programs: A case study. *The International Journal of Management Education*, 15(2): 332–349.

Barnes, A. 2022. Political interference threatens the future of Australian research. *Advocate*, 29(1): 2–3.

Barr, P.S., Stimpert, J.L. and Huff, A.S. 1992. Cognitive change, strategic action, and organizational renewal. *Strategic Management Journal*, 13(S1): 15–36.

Bartel, S. 2018. Leadership barriers for women in higher education. https://www .aacsb.edu/insights/articles/2018/12/leadership-barriers-for-women-in-higher -education

Bartunek, J.M. 2007. Academic–practitioner collaboration need not require joint or relevant research: Towards a relational scholarship of integration. *Academy of Management Journal*, 50: 1323–1333.

Bartunek, J.M. and Rynes, S. 2014. Academics and practitioners are alike and unlike: The paradoxes of academic–practitioner relationships. *Journal of Management*, 40: 1181–1201.

Bayley, J.E. and Phipps, D.P. 2017. Building the concept of research impact literacy. *Evidence and Policy*, 15(4): 597–606.

Bayley J. and Phipps, D. 2020. Impact literacy workbook. https://www.em eraldgrouppublishing.com/sites/default/files/2020-06/Impact%20Literacy% 20Workbook%20Final.pdf

Bayley, J.E., Phipps, D.P. and Batac, M. 2017. Development of a framework for knowledge mobilisation and impact competencies. *Evidence and Policy*, 14(4): 725–738.

Bennington, J. and Moore M.H. (eds) 2011. *Public Value in Complex and Changing Times*. Basingstoke: Palgrave Macmillan.

Benschop, Y.W.M. 2021. Grand challenges, feminist answers. *Organization Theory*, 2(3). https://doi.org/10.1177/26317877211020323

Berry, L.L., Reibstein, D.J., Wijen, F., Van Wassenhove, L., Voss, C., Gustafsson, A., Vereecke, A. and Bolton, R. 2021. Encouraging business scholars to address societal impact. https://www.aacsb.edu/insights/articles/2021/02/encouraging-business-scholars-to-address-societal-impact

Bertassini, A.C., Ometto, A.R., Severengiz, S. and Gerolamo, M.C. 2021. Circular economy and sustainability: The role of organizational behaviour in the transition journey. *Business Strategy and the Environment*, 30(7), 3160–3193.

Betts, M. 2022. How much further from gender equity in higher education did the pandemic take us? Opinion. https://www.campusreview.com.au/2022/03/how-much-further-from-gender-equity-in-higher-education-did-the-pandemic-take-us-opinion/

Bisoux, T. 2021. Elevating the equity curve. AACSB. https://www.aacsb.edu/insights/articles/2021/03/elevating-the-equity-curve

Bobbink, M., Hartmann, A. and Dewulf, G. 2016. Sustaining extended enterprise performance: A value co-creation perspective. *Journal of Organization Design*, 5(3): 1–10.

Bolton, D. and Nie, R.U.I. 2010. Creating value in transnational higher education: The role of stakeholder management. *Academy of Management Learning and Education*, 9(4): 701–714.

Borglund, T., Prenkert, F., Frostenson, M., Helin, S. and Du Rietz, S. 2019. External facilitators as 'Legitimizers' in designing a master's program in sustainable business at a Swedish business school: A typology of industry collaborator roles in RME. *The International Journal of Management Education*, 17(3): 100315.

Borland, H., Ambrosini, V., Lindgreen, A. and Vanhamme, J. 2016. Building theory at the intersection of ecological sustainability and strategic management. *Journal of Business Ethics*, 135(2): 293–307.

Bouchikhi, H. and Kimberly, J. 2016. Quelles stratégies pour les business schools face à la sélection darwinienne en marche? *Le Journal de l'école de Paris du Management*, 119: 38–44.

Boyer, E.L. 1990. *Scholarship Reconsidered: Priorities at the Professoriate*. Princeton, NJ: Carnegie Foundation for the Advancement of Teaching.

Boyer, E. 1996. Scholarship of engagement. *Bulletin of the America Academy of Art and Sciences*, 49: 18–33.

Bozeman, N. and Corley, E. 2004. Scientists' collaboration strategies: Implications for scientific and technical human capital. *Research Policy*, 33(4): 599–616.

Brewer, J.D. (1983). What is social science? In: J.D. Brewer (2013) *The Public Value of the Social Sciences: An Interpretative Essay*. Bloomsbury Collections. (pp. 19–52). London: Bloomsbury Academic.

Bridgeman, T. 2007. Reconstituting relevance exploring possibilities for management educators' critical engagement with the public. *Management Learning*, 38(4): 425–439.

Brocklehurst, M., Sturdy, A., Winstanley, D., and Driver, M. 2007. Introduction: Whither the MBA? Factions, fault lines and the future. *Management Learning*, 38(4): 379–388.

Brown, R.R., Deletic, A. and Wong, T.H.F. (2015) How to catalyse collaboration. *Nature*, 525: 315–317.

Business Schools for Climate Leadership. 2022. Uniting for the planet's future. https://sites.google.com/view/bs4cl/home

CABS. 2021a. https://charteredabs.org/making-the-most-of-the-moment-gender -equality-in-business-and-management-schools/

CABS. 2021b. https://charteredabs.org/chartered-abs-and-itn-launch-business -schools-for-good-film

CABS. 2021c. https://charteredabs.org/wp-content/uploads/2021/06/Chartered -ABS-Business-Schools-and-the-Public-Good-Final-1.pdf

CABS. n.d.a. https://charteredabs.org/research-impact/

CABS n.d.b. https://charteredabs.org/equality-diversity-invisibility-diversity-in -the-business-school-curriculum/

Cagnin, C. 2018. Developing a transformative business strategy through the combination of design thinking and futures literacy. *Technology Analysis and Strategic Management*, 30(5): 524–539.

Calvard, T.S. 2020. *Critical Perspectives on Diversity in Organizations*. London: Routledge.

Campbell, E. 2022. Unacceptable: Melbourne University funding ban over male lineup, https://www.campusreview.com.au/2022/03/unacceptable-melbourne -university-funding-ban-over-male-lineup/

Cassell, C. 2020. On imposters and impact: A comment on the triumph of non-sense. *Academy of Management Learning and Education*, 19(2): 234–235.

Castillo, M.M., Sánchez I.D. and Dueñas-Ocampo, S. 2020. Leaders do not emerge from a vacuum: Toward an understanding of the development of responsible leadership. *Business Society Review*, 125: 329–348.

Cavagnaro, E. and van der Zande, I.S.E. 2021. Reflecting on responsible leadership in the context of higher education, *Journal of Leadership Education*, 20(3): 139–155.

Cheng, M. 2019. 8 characteristics of millennials that support Sustainable Development Goals (SDGs). https://www.forbes.com/sites/margueritacheng/ 2019/06/19/8-characteristics-of-millennials-that-support-sustainable-development -goals-sdgs/?sh=5ff0619b29b7

Connell, R. 2007. *Southern Theory*. Allen & Unwin: Sydney.

Cooke, B. 2003. The denial of slavery in management studies. *Journal of Management Studies*, 40(8): 1895–1918.

Corriveau, A.-M. 2020. Developing authentic leadership as a starting point to responsible management: A Canadian university case study. *The International Journal of Management Education*, 18(1): 100364.

Crenshaw, K. 1989. Demarginalizing the intersection of race and sex: A black feminist critique of antidiscrimination doctrine, feminist theory and anti-racist politics. *University of Chicago Legal Forum*. Available at: http:// chicagounbound.uchicago.edu/uclf/vol1989/iss1/8

Crittenden, V. and Peterson, R.A. 2019. Keeping the marketing curriculum current in an era of digital disruption, *Journal of Marketing Education*, 41(2): 75–76.

Cullen, J.G. 2020. Varieties of responsible management learning: A review, typology and research agenda. *Journal of Business Ethics*, 162: 759–773.

Currie, G., Davies, J. and Ferlie, E. 2016. A call for university-based business schools to 'lower their walls': Collaborating with other academic departments in pursuit of social value. *Academy of Management Learning and Education*, 15(4): 742–755.

Dameron, S. and Durand, T. 2009. 2020Vision: A dual strategy for European Business Schools. *EFMD Global Focus*, 03(1). https://issuu.com/efmd/docs/global-focus-vol-03-issue-01

Davies, J., Yarrow. E., and Syed, J. (2019). The curious under-representation of women impact case leaders: Can we disengender inequality regimes? *Gender, Work and Organization*, 27(2): 129–148.

Dawe, G., Jucker, R. and Martin, S. 2005. Sustainable development in higher education: Current practice and future developments. http://www. heacademy.ac .uk/assets/York/documents/ourwork/tla/sustainability/sustdevinHEfinalreport .pdf

Deane, P. 2021. SDGs are transforming 'global academy' from rhetoric to reality. https://www.timeshighereducation.com/opinion/sdgs-are-transforming-global -academy-rhetoric-reality

Deloitte. 2021. A call for accountability and action. https://www2.deloitte .com/content/dam/Deloitte/global/Documents/2021-deloitte-global-millennial -survey-report.pdf

Dodson, M. 2015. *Towards the Fully Engaged University: The Particularly Australian Challenge.* Manchester, UK: British Council. Global Education Dialogues: Stimulus Paper.

Dyllick, T. 2015. Responsible management education for a sustainable world: The challenges for business schools. *Journal of Management Development*, 34(1): 16–33.

EFMD (European Foundation for Management Development). 2022. EFMD and responsible management. https://www.efmdglobal.org/knowledge/efmd-and -responsible-management/

Elkington, J. 1998. Cannibals with Forks: The Triple Bottom Line of Sustainability. Gabriola Island, BC: New Society Publishers.

Ellis, R. 2021. Talking leadership. https://www.timeshighereducation.com/talking -leadership/talking-leadership3-minouche-shafik-embedding-sustainability? mc_cid=4e70a649a9&mc_eid=059f627f81

Falkner-Rose, L. 2022. *Tell Us: What Are You Doing? Improving How you Communicate your Academic Research, Relevance and Expertise.* ABDC.

Ferlie, E., McGivern, G. and De Moraes, A. 2010. Developing a public interest school of management. *British Journal of Management*, 21: S60–S70.

Financial Times. 2021a. FT Global MBA ranking 2021: Methodology and key. https://www.ft.com/mba-method

Financial Times. 2021b. FT European business schools 2021: Methodology and key. https://www.ft.com/euro-schools-method

Financial Times. 2022. Academic focus limits business schools' contribution to society. https://www.ft.com/content/5953739c-3b94-11ea-b84f-a62c46f39bc2

Finch, D.J., Hamilton, L.K., Baldwin, R. and Zehner, M. 2013. An exploratory study of factors affecting undergraduate employability. *Education+Training*, 55: 681–704.

Fisher, G. 2020. Why every business professor should writer practitioner-focused articles. *Business Horizons*, 63: 417–419.

Fissi, S., Romolini, A., Gori, E. and Contri, M. 2021. The path toward a sustainable green university: The case of the University of Florence. *Journal of Cleaner Production, 279*. https://doi.org/10.1016/j.jclepro.2020.123655

Flynn, P.M., Haynes, K. and Kilgour, M.A. (eds). 2020. *Integrating Gender Equality into Business and Management Education: Lessons Learned and Challenges Remaining*. London: Routledge.

Fraser, G. and Watson, R. 2020. Gender diversifying the business curriculum. AACSB. https://www.aacsb.edu/insights/articles/2020/09/gender-diversifying -the-business-curriculum

Frattini, F. 2021. The acceleration of digitalisation within education as a result of COVID-19. globalfocusmagazine.com/the-acceleration-of-digitalisation -within-education-as-a-result-of-covid-19

Friga, P.N., Bettis, R.A. and Sullivan, R.S. 2003. Changes in graduate management education and new business school strategies for the 21st century. *Academy of Management Learning and Education*, 2(3): 233–249.

Ghoshal, S. 2005. Bad management theories are destroying good management practices. *Academy of Management Learning and Education*, 4(1): 75–91.

Godemann, J., Bebbington, J., Herzig, C. and Moon, J. 2014. Higher education and sustainable development: Exploring possibilities for organisational change. *Accounting, Auditing and Accountability Journal*, 27(2): 218–233.

Govindarajan, V. and Srivastava, A. 2020. What the shift to virtual learning could mean for the future of higher ed. *Harvard Business Review*. https://hbr .org/2020/03/what-the-shift-to-virtual-learning-could-mean-for-the-future-of -higher-ed

GRLI (Globally Responsible Leadership Initiative). 2021a. https://grli.org/about/ global-responsibility/

GRLI. 2021b. https://grli.org/about/

Gröschl, S. and Gabaldon, P. 2018. Business schools and the development of responsible leaders: A proposition of Edgar Morin's transdisciplinarity. *Journal of Business Ethics*, 153(1): 185–195.

Grosser, K. 2021. Gender, business and human rights: Academic activism as critical engagement in neoliberal times. Gender, Work and Organization, 28: 1624–1637.

Grosser, K., Moon, J. and Nelson, J. 2017. Gender, business ethics, and corporate social responsibility: Assessing and refocusing a conversation. Business Ethics Quarterly, 27: 541–567.

Harrington, D. Short, J.C. and Hynes, B. 2015. Changing times for management educators: Rethinking engagement with participatory forms of knowledge production. *Irish Journal of Management*, 34(1): 51–59.

Hibbert, P. and Cunliffe, A. 2015. Responsible management: Engaging moral reflexive practice through threshold concepts. *Journal of Business Ethics*, 127(1): 177–188.

Hodgkinson, G.P. and Rousseau, D. 2009. Bridging the rigour relevance gap in management studies: It's already happening. *Journal of Management Studies*, 46(3): 534–546.

Hofgartner, J. 2021. The digital future of education: 3 insights for business schools' leaders, *Teaching and Training*. https://www.barco.com/en/news/2021-03-02-the-digital-future-of-education

Hogan, O., Charles, M.B. and Kortt, M.A. 2021. A view from the top: Deans on Australian Business Schools. *Economic Papers: A Journal of Applied Economics and Policy*, 40(1): 1–13.

Hommel, M. and Hommel, U. 2020. Casualisation in HE is good for business: Get over it. https://www.universityworldnews.com/post.php?story=20201211110620766

Houldsworth, E., McBain, R., and Brewster, C. 2019. 'One MBA?' How context impacts the development of post-MBA. *European Management Journal*, 37(4): 432–441.

Hunt, S.D. 2008. Book review: *Andrew H. Van de Ven Engaged Scholarship: A Guide for Organizational and Social Research*. Oxford: Oxford University Press.

Hynes, B. and Richardson, I. 2007. Creating an entrepreneurial mindset: Getting the process right for information and communication technology students. In: G. Lowry (ed) *Information Systems and Technology Education: From the University to the Workplace*. Hershey, PA: IGI Global.

Jack, A. 2020. Academic focus limits business schools' contribution to society. https://www.ft.com/content/5953739c-3b94-11ea-b84f-a62c46f39bc2

Jack, A. 2022. Shades of green in business education rankings. https://www.ft.com/content/846322e6-a2f5-4207-a2f3-3a1d02e6dfb3

Jacob, W.J., Sutin, S.E., Weidman, J.C. and Yeagew, J.L. 2015. Community engagement in Higher Education: International and local perspectives. In: W.J. Jacob, S.E. Sutin, J.C. Weidman and J.L. Yeagew (eds) *Community Engagement in Higher Education Policy Reforms and Practice*. Pittsburgh Studies in Comparative and International Education, 3. Rotterdam/Boston/Taipei: Sense Publishers.

Jammulamadaka, N., Faria, A., Jack, G. and Ruggunan, S. 2021. Decolonising management and organisational knowledge (MOK): Praxistical theorising for potential worlds. *Organization*, 28(5): 717–740.

Janke, E.M., Medlin, K. and Holland, B. 2014. *Excellence in Community Engagement and Community-Engaged Scholarship: Honoring the Mosaic of Talents and Stewarding the Standards of High Quality Community-engaged Scholarship*, Vol 2. Institute for Community and Economic Engagement, Office of Research and Economic Development. University of North Carolina at Greensboro.

Jones, S. 2020. Covid-19 is our best chance to change universities for good. https://www.theguardian.com/education/2020/mar/31/covid-19-is-our-best-

chance-to-change-universities-for-good?fbclid=IwAR2r5UEqLbTpg9jKhY
07KU3shBpQ_24uPSE_lm84gCNzToRzpl99GCZc9QM

Joy, S. and Poonamallee, L. 2013. Cross-cultural teaching in globalized management classrooms: Time to move from functionalist to postcolonial approaches? *Academy of Management Learning and Education*, 12(3): 396–413.

Kaplan, A. 2018. A school is a 'building that has four walls ... with tomorrow inside': Toward the reinvention of the business school. *Business Horizons*, 61: 599–608.

Kelan, E.K., and Dunkley Jones, R. 2010. Gender and the MBA. *Academy of Management Learning and Education*, 9(1): 26–43.

Kenworthy-U'Ren, A.L. and Peterson, T.O. 2005. Service learning and management education: Introducing the 'we care' approach. *Academy of Management Learning and Education*, 4: 272–277.

Khurana, R. 2007. *From Higher Aims to Hired Hands: The Social Transformation of American Business Schools and the Unfulfilled Promise of Management as a Profession*. Princeton, NJ: Princeton University Press.

Khurana, R. and Spender, J.C. 2012. Herbert A. Simon on what ails business schools: More than 'a problem in organizational design'. *Journal of Management Studies*, 49: 619–639.

Kim, T. 2017. Academic mobility, transnational identity capital, and stratification under conditions of academic capitalism. *Higher Education*, 73(6): 981–997.

King's College London and Digital Science. 2015. The nature, scale and beneficiaries of research impact. https://www.kcl.ac.uk/policy-institute/assets/ref-impact.pdf

Kitchener, M. 2019. The public value of social science: From manifesto to organizational strategy. In: A. Lindgreen, N. Koenig-Lewis, M. Kitchener, J.D. Brewer, M.H. Moore and T. Meynhardt (eds) *Public Value* (pp. 300–315). London: Routledge.

Kitchener, M. and Delbridge, R. 2020. Lessons from creating a business school for public good: Obliquity, waysetting, and wayfinding in substantively rational change. *Academy of Management Learning and Education*, 19(3): 307–322.

Kothiyal, N., Bell, E. and Clarke, C. 2018. Moving beyond mimicry: Developing hybrid spaces in Indian business schools. *Academy of Management Learning and Education*, 17(2): 137–154.

Krishnamurthy, S. 2020. The future of business education: A commentary in the shadow of the Covid-19 pandemic, *Journal of Business Research*, 117: 1–5.

Kurland, N.B., Michaud, K.E., Best, M., Wohldmann, E., Cox, H., Pontikis, K. and Vasishth, A. 2010. Overcoming silos: The role of an interdisciplinary course in shaping a sustainability network. *Academy of Management Learning and Education*, 9(3): 457–476.

Kurucz, E., Colbert, B. and Marcus, J. 2014. Sustainability as a provocation to rethink management education: Building a progressive educative practice. *Management Learning*, 45(4): 437–457.

Laasch, O. and Moosmayer, D. 2015. Competences for responsible management: A structured literature review. *CRME Working Papers*, 1(2): 1–64.

Laasch, O., Moosmayer, D., Antonacopoulou, E. and Schaltegger, S. 2020. Constellations of transdisciplinary practices: A map and research agenda for the responsible management learning field. *Journal of Business Ethics*, 162: 735–757.

Larsen, N. and Kæseler-Mortensen, J. 2020. What is 'Futures Literacy' and why is it important? On overcoming blind resistance to change and poverty of the imagination, Scenario, Copenhagen Institute for Futures Studies. https://en.unesco.org/futuresliteracy/about

Larson, E.W. and Drexler, J.A. 2010. Project management in real time: A service-learning project. *Journal of Management Education*, 34: 551–573.

Liang, N. and Wang, J. 2004. Implicit mental models in teaching cases: An empirical study of popular MBA cases in the United States and China. *Academy of Management Learning and Education*, 3(4): 397–413.

Lister, A. 2020. https://www.businessbecause.com/news/best-business-schools-for/7175/international-students

Littleton, E. 2022. At the crossroads. https://www.nteu.org.au/policy/workforce_issues/insecure_work/news

Maak, T. and Pless, N. 2006. Responsible leadership in a stakeholder society: A relational perspective. *Journal of Business Ethics*, 66(1): 99–115.

Malkki, K. 2010. Building on Mezirow's theory of transformative learning: Theorizing the challenges to reflection, *Journal of Transformative Education*, 8(1):42–62.

Manchester University. 2020. University to decarbonise its investment portfolio. https://www.staffnet.manchester.ac.uk/bmh/about-fbmh/news-and-events/news/display/?id=24211

Manchester University. 2022. Central Procurement Office. https://www.staffnet.manchester.ac.uk/procurement/

MBA Today. 2022. List of triple accredited business schools 2021. https://www.mba.today/guide/triple-accreditation-business-schools

Mbembe, A.J. 2016. Decolonizing the university: New directions. *Arts and Humanities in Higher Education*, 15(1): 29–45.

McCulloch, A. 2009. The student as co-producer: Learning from public administration about the student-university relationship. *Studies in Higher Education*, 34: 171–183.

McGrath, R.G. 2007. No longer a stepchild: How the management field can come into its own. *Academy of Management Journal*, 50(6): 1365–1378.

McGrath-Champ, S., Gavin, M., Stacey, M. and Wilson, R. 2022. Collaborating for policy impact: Academic-practitioner collaboration in industrial relations research. *Journal of Industrial Relations*. https://doi.org/10.1177%2F00221856221094887

McKiernan, P. and Tsui, A.S. 2019. Responsible management research: A senior scholar legacy in doctoral education. *Academy of Management Learning and Education*, 18(2): 310–313.

McTiernan, S., and Flynn, P.M. 2011. 'Perfect storm' on the horizon for women business school deans? *Academy of Management Learning and Education*, 10(2): 323–339.

Metz, I., Harzing, A-W., and Zyphur, M.J. 2016. Of journal editors and editorial boards: Who are the trailblazers in increasing editorial board gender equality? *British Journal of Management*, 27(4): 712–726.

Mezirow, J. 2000. Learning to think like an adult. Core concepts of transformation theory. In: J. Mezirow and Associates (eds), *Learning as Transformation: Critical Perspectives on a Theory in Progress*, (pp. 3–33). San Francisco, CA: Jossey-Bass.

Miller, R. 2007. Futures literacy: A hybrid strategic scenario method. *Futures*, 39(4): 341–362.

Miller, R. 2010. Futures literacy: Embracing complexity and using the future. *Ethos*, 10(10): 23–28.

Miller, R. 2018. Transforming the future, anticipating the 21st century. UNESCO digital library. https://unesdoc.unesco.org/ark:/48223/pf0000264644

Mohanty, C.T. 2003. *Feminism without Borders: Decolonizing Theory, Practising Solidarity*. Durham, NC: Duke University Press.

Moon, C.J., Walmsley, A., and Apostolopoulos, N. 2018. Governance implications of the UN higher education sustainability initiative. *Corporate Governance: The International Journal of Business in Society*, 18(4): 624–634.

Moore, M.H. 2013. *Recognizing Public Value*. Cambridge, MA: Harvard University Press.

Moosmayer, D.C. 2012. A model of management academics' intentions to influence values. *Academy of Management Learning and Education*, 11(2): 155–173.

Moratis, L. and Melissen, F. 2021. Bolstering responsible management education through the sustainable development goals: three perspectives. *Management Learning*, 53(2). https://doi.org/10.1177/1350507621990993.

Moratis, L. and Melissen, F. 2022. Are business schools talking the walk? https://www.globalfocusmagazine.com/are-business-schools-talking-the-walk/

Moreton-Robinson, A. 2015. *The White Possessive: Property, Power, and Indigenous Sovereignty*. Minneapolis: University of Minnesota Press.

Morin, E. 2014. *Enseigner à Vivre. Manifeste pour changer l'éducation*. Paris: Actes Sud.

Morrissey, C. 2019. The digital transformation of management education, faculty perspective, *Graziadio Business Review*, 22(1). https://gbr.pepperdine.edu/2019/03/digital-transformation-of-management-education.

Morsing, M. (ed). 2021. *Responsible Management Education*. Routledge.

Moser, B. 2021. Building sustainability into the German program: "Climate stories" in Gen-Ed German and the advanced curriculum. *Die Unterrichtspraxis/Teaching German*, 54: 257–270.

Mtawa, N.N., Fongwa, N.S. and Wangenge-Ouma, G. 2016. The scholarship of university–community engagement: Interrogating Boyer's model. *International Journal of Educational Development*, 49: 126–133.

Muff, K. 2013. Developing globally responsible leaders in business schools A vision and transformational practice for the journey ahead. *Journal of Management Development*, 32(5): 487–507.

Muff, K., Liechti, A. and Dyllick, T. 2020. How to apply responsible leadership theory in practice: A competency tool to collaborate on the sustainable development goals. *Corporate Social Responsibility and Environmental Management*, 27(5): 2254–2274.

Murillo, D. and Vallentin, S. 2016. The business school's right to operate: Responsibilization and resistance. *Journal of Business Ethics*, 136: 743–757.

Nkomo, S.M. 2015. Challenges for management and business education in a 'developmental' state: The case of South Africa. *Academy of Management Learning and Education*, 14(2): 242–258.

Nkomo, S.M., Bell, M.P., Roberts, L.M., Joshi, A. and Thatcher, S.M.B. 2019. Diversity at a critical juncture: Nee theories for a complex phenomenon. *Academy of Management Review*, 44(3): 498–517.

Nonet, G., Kassel, K. and Meijs, L. 2016. Understanding responsible management: Emerging themes and variations from European business school programs. *Journal of Business Ethics*, 139(4): 717–736.

NTNU (National Tertiary Education Union) (2022) Casuals and insecure work. https://www.nteu.org.au/policy/workforce_issues/insecure_work

Oliver, C. 1991. Strategic responses to institutional processes. *Academy of Management Review*, 16: 145–179.

Oliver, K. and Cairney, P. 2019. The dos and don'ts of influencing policy: A systematic review of advice to academics. *Palgrave Communications*, 5(1).

O'Meara, K., Eatman, T. and Petersen, S. (2015). Advancing engaged scholarship in promotion and tenure: A roadmap and call for reform. *Liberal Education*, 101(3): n3.

Ortiz, D. and Huber-Heim, K. 2017. From information to empowerment: Teaching sustainable business development by enabling an experiential and participatory problem-solving process in the classroom. *The International Journal of Management Education*, 15: 318–331.

O'Shea, S.C. 2017. This girl's life: An autoethnography. *Organization*, 25(1): 3–20.

Ozturk, M.B. and Rumens, N. 2014. Gay male academics in UK business and management schools: Negotiating heteronormativities in everyday worklife. *British Journal of Management*, 25: 503–517.

Parker, L.D. 2013. Contemporary university strategizing: The financial imperative. *Financial Accountability and Management*, 29(1): 1–25.

Parker, M. 2018. *Shut Down the Business School! An Insider's Account of What's Wrong with Management Education*. London: Pluto Press.

Paucar-Caceres, A., Cavalcanti-Bandos, M.F., Quispe-Prieto, S.C., Huerta-Tantalean, L.N. and Werner-Masters, K. 2021. Using soft systems methodology to align community projects with sustainability development in higher education stakeholders' networks in a Brazilian university. *Systems Research Behavioral Science*. https://doi.org/10.1002/sres.2818

Perriton, L., Elliott, C. and Humbert, A.L. (2022) Where is the visible commitment to gender in the advertised content of UK management degree programmes? Gender in Management: An International Journal, 37 (1): 58–76.

Pettigrew, A.M. and Starkey, K. 2016. The legitimacy and impact of business schools: Key issues and a research agenda. *Academy of Management Learning and Education*, 15(4): 649–664.

Pfeffer, J. and Fong, C.T. 2012. The end of business schools? Less success that meets the eyes. *Academy of Management Learning and Education*, 1: 78–95.

Phillips, M., Pullen, A. and Rhodes, C. 2014. Writing organization as gendered practice: Interrupting the libidinal economy. *Organization Studies*, 35(3): 313–333.

Pless, N.M., Maak, T. and Stahl, G.K. 2011. Developing responsible global leaders through international service-learning programs: The Ulysses experience. *Academy of Management Learning and Education*, 10(2): 237–260.

Porritt, J. 2005. Capitalism as if the World Matters. London: Earthscan.

Prahalad, C.K. and Ramaswamy, V. 2004. Co-creation experiences: The next practice in value creation. *Journal of Interactive Marketing*, 18(3): 5–14.

Price, A. and Delbridge, R. 2015. *Social Science Parks: Society's New Super Labs*. London: Nesta.

Rasche, A. and Escudero, M. 2010. Leading change: the role of the principles of responsible management education. *Journal of Business and Economic Ethics* 10(2): 244–250.

Rasche, A. and Kell, G. (eds) 2010. *The United Nations Global Compact: Achievements, Trends and Challenges*. Cambridge: Cambridge University Press.

Rasche, A., Ulrich, G.D. and Schedel, I. 2012. Cross-disciplinary ethics education in MBA programs: Rhetoric or reality? *Academy of Management Learning and Education*, 12(1): 71–85.

Renwick, D.W.S., Jabbour, C.J.C., Muller-Camen, M., Redman, T. and Wilkinson, A. 2016. Contemporary developments in green (environmental) HRM scholarship. *The International Journal of Human Resource Management*, 27(2): 114–128.

Renwick, K., Selkrig, M., Manathunga, C. and Keamy, R. 2020. Community engagement is …: Revisiting Boyer's model of scholarship. *Higher Education Research and Development*, 39(2): 1232–1246.

Rial, J.F. 2021a. Il faut sortir du tourisme de masse. https://www.lexpress.fr/styles/mobilite/jean-francois-rial-il-faut-sortir-du-tourisme-de-masse_2150386.html

Rial, J.F. 2021b. Le tourisme durable n'est plus un objectif mais bien une necessité absolue. https://www.tourmag.com/Le-tourisme-durable-n-est-plus -un-objectif-mais-bien-une-necessite-absolue-selon-J-F-Rial_a109501.html

Rickards, L., Steele, W., Kokshagina, O. and Moraes, O. 2020. *Research Impact as Ethos*. Melbourne: RMIT University.

Roberts, L.M. and Mayo, A.J. 2019. Toward a racially just workplace. *Harvard Business Review*. https://hbr.org/2019/11/toward-a-racially-just-workplace

Robinson, S. 2006. Reflecting on the international group working experience: A study of two MBA programmes. *International Journal of Management Education*, 5(2): 3–14.

Rubin, R.S. and Dierdorff, E.C. 2013. Building a better MBA: From a decade of critique toward a decennium of creation. *Academy of Management Learning and Education*, 2(1): 125–141.

Rusinko, C.A. 2010. Integrating sustainability in management and business education: A matrix approach. *Academy of Management Learning and Education*, 9(3): 507–519.

Ryazanova, O. and McNamara, P. 2019. Choices and consequences: Impact of mobility on research-career capital and promotion in business schools. *Academy of Management Learning and Education*, 18(2): 186–212.

Rynes, S.L. 2017. Academy of Management Journal Editors' Forum on the Research–Practice Gap in Human Resource Management, Editor's Foreword: Tackling the 'great divide' between research production and dissemination in human resource management. *Academy of Management Journal*, 50(5): 985–986.

Rynes, S.L., Bartunek, J.M. and Daft, R.L. 2001. Across the great divide: Knowledge creation and transfer between practitioners and academics. *The Academy of Management Journal*, 44(2): 340–355.

Rynes, S.L., McNatt, B. and Bretz, R.D. 1999. Academic research inside organizations: Inputs, processes and outcomes. *Personnel Psychology*, 52: 869–898.

Samson, D., Donnet, T., and Daft, R.L. 2021. *Management* (7th edn). Melbourne: Cengage Learning Australia.

Sandmann, L., Saltmarsh, J. and O'Meara, K. 2016. An integrated model for advancing the scholarship of engagement: Creating academic homes for the engaged scholar. *Journal of Higher Education Outreach and Engagement*, 20(1): 157–174.

Savage, E., Tapics, T., Evarts, J. and Tirone, S. 2015. Experiential learning for sustainability leadership in higher education. *International Journal of Sustainability in Higher Education*, 16(5): 692–705.

Savaget, P., Geissdoerfer, M., Kharrazi, A. and Evans, S. 2019. The theoretical foundations of sociotechnical systems change for sustainability: A systematic literature review. *Journal of Cleaner Production*, 206: 878–892.

Savigny, H. 2020. The violence of impact: Unpacking relations between gender, media and politics. *Political Studies Review*, 18(2): 277–293.

Schlegelmilch, B. 2020. Why business schools need radical innovations: Drivers and development trajectories. *Journal of Marketing Education*, 42(2): 93–107.

Shapiro, D.L. and Kirkman, B. 2018. It's time to make business school research more relevant. *Harvard Business Review*. https://hbr.org/2018/07/its-time-to-make-business-school-research-more-relevant

Sharma, G. and Bansal, P. 2020. Co-creating rigorous and relevant knowledge. *Academy of Management Journal*, 63: 386–410.

Shrivastava, P. 2010. Pedagogy of passion for sustainability. *Academy of Management Learning and Education*, 9(3): 443–455.

Simsek, Z., Bansal, P., Shaw, J.D., Heugens, P. and Smith, W. 2018. From the editors—Seeing practice impact in new ways. *Academy of Management Journal*, 61(6): 2021–2025.

Skiles, M., Yang, E., Reshef, O., Muñoz, D.R., Cintron, D., Lind, M.L., Rush, A., Calleja, P.P., Nerenberg, R., Armani, A. and Faust, K.M., 2022. Conference demographics and footprint changed by virtual platforms. *Nature Sustainability*, 5: 149–156.

Smit, A. 2013. Responsible leadership development through management education: A business ethics perspective. *African Journal of Business Ethics*, 7(2), Conference Edition: 45–51.

Smyth, J. 2020. Australian business schools: Will overseas students return? https://www.ft.com/content/3945156a-6e08-4231-bf26-f8a576f07584

Solitander, N., Fougere, M., Sobczak, A. and Herlin, H. 2012. We are the champions: Organizational learning and change for responsible management education. *Journal of Management Education*, 36(3): 337–363.

Starik, M., Rands, G., Marcus, A.A. and Clark, T.S. 2010. From the guest editors: In search of sustainability in management education. *Academy of Management Learning and Education*, 9(3): 377–383.

Starkey, K. and Madan, P. 2001. Bridging the relevance gap: Aligning stakeholders in the future of management research. *British Journal of Management*, 12: S3–S26.

Stokes, J. and Dopson, S. 2020. From ego to eco: Leadership for the Fourth Industrial Revolution. www.SBS.Oxford.edu/custom

Stremersch, S., Winer, R.S. and Camacho, N. 2022. Faculty research incentives and business school health: a new perspective from and for marketing. *Journal of Marketing*. https://doi.org/10.1177%2F00222429211001050

Sturdy, A. and Gabriel, Y. 2000. Missionaries, mercenaries, or car salesmen? MBA teaching in Malaysia. *Journal of Management Studies*, 37(7): 97–1002.

Suddaby, R., Coraiola, D., Harvey, C. and Foster, W. 2020. History and the micro-foundations of dynamic capabilities. *Strategic Management Journal*, 41(3): 530–556.

Symonds, M. 2021. https://www.forbes.com/sites/mattsymonds/2021/11/10/how-can-business-schools-help-to-save-the-planet/?sh=43ed1c1343d7

Tadaki, M., Salmond, J. and Heron, R.L. 2014. Applied climatology: Doing the relational work of climate. *Progress in Physical Geography*, 38(4): 392–413.

Thangaiah, E.A., Jenal, R. and Yahaya, J. 2021. Integration of value co-creation into the e-learning platform. *International Journal of Advanced Computer Science and Applications*, 12(9): 153–159.

Thomas, H. and Starkey, K. 2019. The future of business schools: Shut them down or broaden our horizons. https://www.globalfocusmagazine.com/the-future-of-business-schools-shut-them-down-or-broaden-our-horizons/

Thomas, L. and Ambrosini, V. 2021. The future role of the business school: A value cocreation perspective. *Academy of Management Learning and Education*, 20(2): 249–269.

Thomas, L., Billsberry, J., Ambrosini, V. and Barton, H. 2014. Convergence and divergence dynamics in British and French business schools: How will the pressure for accreditation influence these dynamics? *British Journal of Management*, 25(2): 305–319.

Thompson, L. 2010. The global moral compass for business leaders. *Journal of Business Ethics*, 93(S1): 15–32.

Tienari, J. and Taylor, S. 2019. Feminism and men: Ambivalent space for acting up. *Organization*, 26(6): 948–960.

Times Higher Education. 2021. Impact Rankings 2021: Methodology. https://www.timeshighereducation.com/world-university-rankings/impact-rankings-2021-methodology

Tourish, D. 2019. *Management Studies in Crisis: Fraud, Deception and Meaningless Research*. Cambridge: Cambridge University Press.

Tourish, D. 2020. The triumph of nonsense in management studies. *Academy of Management Learning and Education*, 19(1): 99–109.

Trank, C.Q. and Rynes, S.L. 2003. Who moved our cheese? Reclaiming professionalism in business education. *Academy of Management Learning and Education*, 2(2): 189–205.

Tremblay, K., Lalancette, L. and Roseveare, 2012. *Assessment of Higher Education Learning Outcomes Feasibility Study Report, Volume 1 – Design and Implementation*, OECD.

Tripsas, M. and Gavetti, G. 2000. Capabilities, cognition, and inertia: Evidence from digital imaging. *Strategic Management Journal*, 21(10–11): 1147–1161.

Tufano, P. 2020. A bolder vision for business schools. https://hbr.org/2020/03/a-bolder-vision-for-business-schools

Tullis, K.J. and Camey, J.P. 2007. Strategic implications of specialized business school accreditation: End of the line for some business education programs? *Journal of Education for Business*, 83(1): 45–51.

UCEA (Universities and Colleges Employers Association). 2021. Examining the gender pay gap in HE. https://www.ucea.ac.uk/library/infographics/gender-pay/

ULSF (University Leaders for a Sustainable Future). 2022a. https://ulsf.org/about/

ULSF. 2022b. https://ulsf.org/talloires-declaration/

Uncles, M.D. 2018. Directions in higher education: A marketing perspective. *Australasian Marketing Journal*, 26: 187–193.

UNESCO (United Nations Educational, Scientific and Cultural Organization). 2021. Futures Literacy: An essential competency for the 21st century, https://en.unesco.org/futuresliteracy/about

UNESCO.org. https://en.unesco.org/themes/education-sustainable-development/what-is-esd/un-decade-of-esd

UN Global Compact. 2021a.

UN Global Compact. 2021b. https://www.unglobalcompact.org/what-is-gc

UN Global Compact. 2021c. https://sdgs.un.org/goals

UN Global Compact. 2021d. https://www.unglobalcompact.org/what-is-gc/mission

University of Birmingham. 2022. University of Birmingham becomes first university to mainstream climate change into accountancy course. https://www.birmingham.ac.uk/news/2022/university-of-birmingham-becomes-first-university-to-mainstream-climate-change-into-accountancy-course-1#

UNPRME. 2021a. https://www.unprme.org/how-to-engage

UNPRME. 2021b. https://www.unprme.org/about

UNPRME. 2021c. https://www.unprme.org/what-we-do

USAID. 2013. Education: The most powerful weapon for changing the world. Impact blog. https://blog.usaid.gov/2013/04/education-the-most-powerful-weapon/#:~:text=As%20Nelson%20Mandela%20says%2C%20%E2%80%9CEducation, illness%2C%20and%20to%20fostering%20peace

Vakkayil, J. and Chatterjee, D. 2017. Globalization routes: The pursuit of conformity and distinctiveness by top business schools in India. *Management Learning*, 48(3): 328–344.

Van der Brugge, R. and Van Raak, R. 2007. Facing the adaptive management challenge: Insights from transition management. *Ecology and Society*, 12(2): 33 (online).

Van de Ven, A.H. 2007. *Engaged Scholarship: A Guide for Organizational and Social Research*. New York: Oxford University Press.

Van de Ven, A. 2011. Engaged scholarship stepping out, *Business Strategy Review*, 22(2): 43–45.

Van de Ven, A.H. and Johnson, P.E. 2006. Knowledge for theory and practice. *Academy of Management Review*, 31: 802–821.

Verbos, A.K. and Humphries, M. 2015. *Business and Society Review*, 120, 23–56.

Voegtlin, C, Frisch, C., Walther, A. and Schwab, P. 2020. Theoretical development and empirical examination of a three-roles model of responsible leadership, *Journal of Business Ethics*, 167: 411–431.

Watson, J. 2003. *Media Communication: An Introduction to Theory and Process* (2nd edn). Basingstoke: Palgrave.

Watson, A. and Huntington, O. 2014. Transgressions of the man on the moon: Climate change, Indigenous expertise, and the posthumanist ethics of place and space. *GeoJournal*, 79(6): 721–736.

WCED (World Commission on Environment and Development). 1987. Our Common Future: Report of the World Commission on Environment and Development. Ed. G.H. Brundtland. Oxford: Oxford University Press.

Westwood, R.I. and Jack, G. 2009. *International and Cross-Cultural Management Studies: A Postcolonial Reading*. Basingstoke: Palgrave Macmillan.

Weybrecht, G. 2022. Business schools need to get serious about sustainability. https://www.ft.com/content/dc056f5f-2744-485e-a67f-362418c9375f

Wharton. 2022. Wharton social impact initiative. https://socialimpact.wharton.upenn.edu

Wickert, C., Post, C., Doh, J.P., Prescott, J.E. and Prencipe, A. 2021. Management research that makes a difference: Broadening the meaning of impact. *Journal of Management Studies*, 58(2): 297–320.

Williams, K. 2022. *Historical Female Management Theorists: Frances Perkins, Hallie Flanagan, Madeleine Parent, Viola Desmond*. Emerald Publishing.

Winter, J. and Cotton, D. 2012. Making the hidden curriculum visible: Sustainability literacy in higher education. *Environmental Education Research*, 18(6): 783–796.

Wittenberg-Cox, A. 2020. Business schools are balancing at last. https://www.forbes.com/sites/avivahwittenbergcox/2020/03/02/business-schools-are-balancing-at-last/?sh=547c1ae51599

World Economic Forum. 2021. UN Sustainable Development Goals: How companies stack up. https://www.weforum.org/agenda/2021/03/how-aligned-are-un-companies-with-their-sustainable-development-goals/

World Health Organization. 2005 Resolution WHA58.34. Ministerial summit on health research. In: Fifty-Eighth World Health Assembly, Geneva, 16–25 May 2005. Geneva: World Health Organization. https://apps.who.int/gb/ebwha/pdf_files/WHA58-REC1/english/A58_2005_REC1-en.pdf

Wright, S. 2019. Towards an affective politics of hope: Learning from land struggles in the Philippines. *Environment and Planning E: Nature and Space.* doi .org/10.1177/2514848619867613

Wright, S., Plahe, J. and Jack, G. 2022. Feeling climate change to the bone: emotional topologies of climate. *Third World Quarterly.* doi.org/10.1080/ 01436597.2021.1987210

Yousafzai, S. 2021. Women in higher education still hold fewer leadership positions and earn less than their male counterparts. How can female academics achieve equity? https://www.aacsb.edu/insights/articles/2022/04/glass-ceiling -sticky-floor

Zizka, L., McGunagle, M and Clark, P.J. 2021. Sustainability in science, technology, engineering and mathematics (STEM) programs: Authentic engagement through a community-based approach. *Journal of Cleaner Production,* 279(10): 123715.

Zlotkowski, E. 1996. Opportunity for All: Linking service-learning and business education. *Journal of Business Ethics*, 15: 5–19.

Index

Printed and bound by CPI Group (UK) Ltd, Croydon, CR0 4YY

07/05/2024

14499073-0001